Ten-Minute Plays

VOLUME IV

FOR KIDS: COMEDY

10+ Format

Ten-Minute Plays

VOLUME IV

FOR KIDS

• • •

COMEDY

10+ Format

YOUNG ACTORS SERIES

Kristen Dabrowski

A Smith and Kraus Book

A Smith and Kraus Book
Published by Smith and Kraus, Inc.
177 Lyme Road, Hanover, NH 03755
www.SmithandKraus.com

First Edition: April 2006
10 9 8 7 6 5 4 3 2 1
Manufactured in the United States of America

Cover and text design by Julia Hill Gignoux, Freedom Hill Design

ISBN 1-57525-441-7
Ten-Minute Plays for Kids Series ISSN 1553-0477

CONTENTS

TO THE DRAMA CLUB
for inspiring me and testing out my ideas:

Alisha, Anabel, Bella, Dan, Dani,
Devon, Ellie, Emily, Harris, Jared, Jordan,
Kelley, Louise, Matthew, Olivia, Pansy,
Sam, Sarah, Sophie, Toni Whitney, William, Zachary

INTRODUCTION

Ten-Minute Plays aims to score on many playing fields. This book contains twelve short plays. Each play then contains two scenes and four monologues. Add it up! That means that this book contains twelve plays, twenty-four scenes, and forty-eight monologues. There's a lot to choose from, but it's not overwhelming. The plays and scenes are marked clearly. Note that the text for the monologues is set in a different typeface. If you are working on a monologue and are not performing the play or scene as a whole, take the time to hear in your mind any additional lines or character responses that you need for the monologue to make sense.

Beat indicates there is a dramatic pause in the action. You will want to consider why the beat is there. Does no one know what to do? Is someone thinking?

Feel free to combine characters (so fewer actors are needed), change a character from male to female (or vice versa), or alter the text in any way that suits you. Be as creative as you like!

For each play, I've included tips for young actors and ideas for playwrights. Here's a guide to the symbols:

    🎭 = tips for actors

    ✍ = ideas for playwrights

There's a lot to work with here. Actors, the tips are meant to give you some guidance and information on how to be an even finer actor. Playwrights, I've included a few of my inspirations and invite you to borrow from them to write your own plays.

At the end of each play is a section called "Talk Back!" with discussion questions. These questions are catalysts for class discussions and projects. The plays do not make moral judgments. They are intended to spark students to use their imaginations and create their own code of ethics. Even if you're not in school, "Talk Back!" can give you some additional ideas and interesting subjects to discuss.

Lastly, there are four extras in the Appendix: Character Questionnaire for Actors, Playwright's Checklist, Scene Elements Worksheet, and Exploration Games. Each activity adds dimension and depth to the plays and is intended to appeal to various learning styles.

Enjoy!

Kristen Dabrowski

The Stain

3F, 2M

WHO

FEMALES	MALES
Jody	Andy
Libby	James
Sandy	

WHERE In school.

WHEN Afternoon, present day.

🎭 See how different and clear you can make your character from the others. How is James different from Andy? Each character is very individual!

✍ This play is about embarrassment at school. See if you can write a short play on this topic. I could probably write twenty-seven!

Scene 1: The Pants

SANDY: You're late!

ANDY: I know, I know!

SANDY: Where were you?

ANDY: I'm having a really bad day. I missed the bus and had to walk to school. And when I was walking to school, it started raining. And after it started raining, a car drove by and got me soaking wet. And then . . . Well, it's been a really lousy day, Sandy. What did I miss? Did Mrs. Ashcroft ever find that spider we put in her desk? It's got to be dead by now. Poor Spidey. He didn't deserve to die so young. Why do you girls think that spiders are scary even though they're, like, smaller than your smallest toe? I totally don't get that. Girls don't make any sense. *(Beat.)* Hey, how great is it that I got to school just in time for lunch today? My day is looking up!

SANDY: You smell funny.

ANDY: Thanks a lot.

SANDY: You're welcome.

ANDY: I was being sarcastic.

SANDY: I know. I'm smarter than you—remember?

(JODY enters.)

JODY: Anyone seen my lunch?

SANDY: Nope.

ANDY: Nope.

JODY: What's that smell?

SANDY: Andy.

JODY: Andy? How come you smell?

ANDY: A car drove by me, getting me soaking wet—-

SANDY: And?

JODY: I don't get it.

ANDY: I wasn't done talking. The car that drove by me, getting me soaking wet, also drove over a skunk.

JODY: You got sprayed by a skunk?

SANDY: That's disgusting.

ANDY: I *know*.

JODY: P.U.!

ANDY: *(To Sandy.)* I told you I was having a bad day.

SANDY: Sounds like the worst day ever.

JODY: So nobody saw my lunch, right?

SANDY: No. And I am outta here! You smell, Andy.

ANDY: I *know*!

JODY: Help me find my lunch!

SANDY: What's in your lunch?

JODY: An egg salad sandwich, chocolate pudding—-

SANDY: Yum! If I find it, can I have your pudding?

JODY: No way!

(SANDY and JODY exit.)

ANDY: I'm hungry.

(JAMES enters.)

JAMES: Hey, how come you're sitting alone?

ANDY: I smell.

JAMES: So?

ANDY: So, that's why.

JAMES: Oh. (JAMES sits next to ANDY.) How come you just got to school?

ANDY: Long story.

JAMES: Oh. Well, you missed a great math class.

ANDY: Really? Well, that just figures. Every day there's a boring math class. And the one day I get to school late—

JAMES: I was kidding. It was totally boring.

ANDY: Oh. Good.

JAMES: I wish I got to school late. I hate school.

ANDY: Me, too.

JAMES: You do smell.

ANDY: I know.

JAMES: What is that smell?

ANDY: Skunk.

JAMES: How come you didn't change?

ANDY: 'Cause I was gonna miss the bus.

JAMES: So, if you got the bus, why are you late?

ANDY: Because I missed the bus anyway.

JAMES: So why didn't you go home?

ANDY: Because the last time I missed the bus, I went home and my mom got really mad at me.

JAMES: Oh.

ANDY: Yeah. Worst day ever.

JAMES: Every day is the worst day ever for me.

ANDY: I wouldn't be so sure.

JAMES: How come you're not eating lunch?

ANDY: A dog ate it.

JAMES: Seriously?

ANDY: Yeah.

JAMES: When?

ANDY: After the skunk sprayed me, I took a shortcut through somebody's yard.

JAMES: And they had a dog.

ANDY: Right. Who chased me.

JAMES: And ate your lunch.

ANDY: Yeah.

JAMES: Man, that's really bad.

ANDY: I know. I'm hungry.

JAMES: Well, I gotta go. I'm gonna play baseball.

ANDY: Can I play, too?

JAMES: Sure.

(ANDY and JAMES stand up.)

ANDY: I feel weird.

JAMES: Why?

(JODY and SANDY enter.)

SANDY: We still can't find Jody's lunch.

ANDY: Um, I think I found it.

JODY: Where?

ANDY: (Pointing to his backside.) Here. I sat on it.

JODY: Gross!

SANDY: I don't want your pudding anymore.

JODY: Neither do I!

JAMES: Ha, ha! It's stuck to your pants!

ANDY: I am the unluckiest person on the planet. Why can't anything go right for me? Everyone's going to laugh at me. I'm ruined. This is a disaster. I have to sit through the rest of school with dirty water, skunk spray, egg salad, and chocolate pudding on my pants! (Beat.) They won't let me go home, will they? Of course they won't! Because that would be good, and nothing good ever happens to me. Jeez, oh man! I have to find a way to keep my dignity. I've got to pull myself together. I can't let a little stain get in my way, right? Maybe everyone will leave me alone for the rest of the day. It'll be nice. Peaceful. I bet the teachers won't even ask me any questions. They'll feel sorry for me! This is going to be a great day! I love this day!

SANDY: You've lost your mind.

JODY: You smell awful!

JAMES: You've got a huge stain on your butt!

ANDY: I *know*!

Scene 2: The Test

(ANDY *sits alone.*)

ANDY: Stupid social studies! No one said there was a test. Teacher didn't say so. How can everyone else know about it but me? I pay attention!

(LIBBY *enters.*)

LIBBY: You're talking to yourself.

ANDY: Did you know about the test?

LIBBY: Uh-huh.

ANDY: How did you know?

LIBBY: Teacher said so yesterday.

ANDY: When?

LIBBY: In class.

ANDY: I didn't hear it.

LIBBY: I did.

ANDY: Stupid social studies!

LIBBY: It's just a test. Take it easy.

ANDY: I can't!

LIBBY: So why are you here?

ANDY: Nobody came to pick me up. I'll probably be here forever.

LIBBY: I don't think so. I don't think you could be here forever.

ANDY: I didn't mean—

LIBBY: I think at some point *someone* will pick you up from school, Andy. They'll probably remember when it's time to eat dinner. Don't they yell at you to do your homework and go to bed? Because they might remember then. Besides, even if they didn't pick you up ever, you can only go to school for so many years. Unless you're dumb and you have to take the same grade over and over again. I can see you being really old with liver spots and no hair, still sitting right here, waiting to get picked up from school. Moaning just like now. "Oh, what a bad day! I didn't know about the test! Poor me! Nobody loves me!" And you'll be wearing those same smelly pants with the stain, only they smell even worse because you've been wearing them forever, and there's a hole in the butt because you've gotten bigger and fatter and split them. I feel so sorry for you.

ANDY: Shut up already! Thanks a lot. That's great. Now I feel really bad.

LIBBY: I'm sorry, but you need to be prepared. Maybe you should just drop out of school now and get a job.

ANDY: People don't give jobs to kids.

LIBBY: They might.

ANDY: It's against the law.

LIBBY: People break the law all the time.

ANDY: So you're saying I should quit school and work for criminals.

LIBBY: Well, you've only been in school a few years. It's not like you can be a doctor or anything.

ANDY: Well, maybe I'll go to Africa to be a photographer.

LIBBY: You don't have a camera.

ANDY: I'll get one.

LIBBY: No, you won't.

ANDY: How do you know?

LIBBY: I know.

ANDY: No, you don't.

LIBBY: Yes, I do.

ANDY: No, you don't.

LIBBY: You smell.

ANDY: I *know*!

LIBBY: No one's going to give you a camera.

ANDY: I'll buy one.

LIBBY: You don't have a job, remember?

ANDY: I'll steal one.

LIBBY: See? I told you you'd be a criminal.

ANDY: I'm not old enough to be a criminal!

LIBBY: Sure, you are.

ANDY: Listen, someone's going to pick me up from school.

LIBBY: Good.

ANDY: Any time now.

LIBBY: Right. *(Beat.)* Unless they forgot. *(Beat.)* Or if they don't like you.

ANDY: My parents like me!

LIBBY: Don't get mad. I didn't do anything.

ANDY: You're annoying.

LIBBY: That hurt my feelings.

ANDY: Well, I'm sorry, but you're really depressing, Libby. And you're a know-it-all.

LIBBY: I was just trying to be nice.

ANDY: Well, you weren't being nice. **What's it like to be perfect and know *everything*, Libby? Because to me it seems obnoxious and boring. To me, it seems like** a stupid waste of my time. I'm already thinking that I'm going to be stuck at school forever. I'm aware of that possibility. I don't want to think about it. I don't want to walk home in the rain. I hate walking home. But I'm trying to be positive here, and you do nothing but make me feel bad. *(Beat.)* Now you're pouting like *I* did something mean. Give me a break, Libby. *You're* the pain in the butt here. I was just sitting here minding my own business. *You* came by and started talking to me. *You* told me I smell and that no one likes me, *which is not true.* Why don't you just go away and bug someone else? I've got my own problems and I don't need you making them worse. I'm having a bad day: I have a stain on my pants, I smell because of it, I'm stuck at school, and I don't need you reminding me of all of it!

(LIBBY turns her back on ANDY. Beat.)

LIBBY: You hurt my feelings. You're a jerk.

ANDY: If you didn't—-

LIBBY: Don't talk to me, Stain Boy!

ANDY: Don't call me Stain Boy!

LIBBY: OK, Stain Boy.

ANDY: I'm not Stain Boy.

LIBBY: You're Stain Boy forever.

ANDY: Am not!

LIBBY: Are too! You're Stinky Stain Boy!

(ANDY stands and walks over to LIBBY.)

ANDY: Take it back!

(LIBBY screams and runs away.)

ANDY: I just need to go home now! This day has to end!

(LIBBY pops her head back in.)

LIBBY: The gym teacher found some shorts for you to wear. *Girl shorts.* Size extra small.

ANDY: You're kidding. And it's not funny.

LIBBY: Yes, it is.

ANDY: No, it's not.

LIBBY: Yes, it is.

ANDY: So, you're kidding, right?

LIBBY: Nope!

(LIBBY exits.)

ANDY: Aaaaaah! I *hate* this day!

TALK BACK!

1. How would you handle a situation like Andy's?

2. What do you do if other kids make fun of you?

3. What *should* you do if other kids make fun of you?

4. Do you ever feel powerless? Why?

5. What is dignity? Do you have it?

6. Which character is most like you? Why?

7. Which character is least like you? Why?

CHICKEN WARRIOR

3F, 3M

WHO

FEMALES	MALES
Emily	Joe
Marjorie	Ty
Violet	Walt

WHERE Walt's farm.

WHEN Daytime, present day.

🎭 Think about how you can make the action seem real. You can't use real chickens so you must act as though they are there!

✍ For this play, I picked two random words out of a hat and came up with a title. Then I had to think of what I could write that would match the title. Try it!

Scene 1: Plan A

(WALT speaks offstage to his mother. We do not see or hear her.)

WALT: That's a girl's job! I don't want to do it! Mom, don't make me. Can't *you* do it? It's not fair! Gathering eggs—that's girl stuff. *(Beat.)* I don't know why; it just is! Guys plow fields, chop wood, and drive tractors. Girls milk cows and gather eggs and stuff. What if I don't do it? I might not. I don't want to. What will you do then? Should I go to my room now? I like my room. I don't care. So go ahead. Ground me. *(Beat.)* Fine! I'll get the stupid eggs. But if they all break, it's not my fault! I hate chickens! I hate chicken poop! I hate everything! OK, chickens, here I come!

(MARJORIE enters.)

MARJORIE: Whatcha doin', Walt? How come you're yelling?

WALT: I have to get stupid eggs from stupid chickens.

MARJORIE: Oh.

WALT: Actually, chickens aren't so bad, are they?

MARJORIE: No. Not really. They are kind of cute. Not bunny cute, but not totally ugly.

WALT: Yeah. Chickens are great. Really . . . cute. So . . . wanna gather some eggs?

MARJORIE: No.

WALT: Now, eggs—they're really cute. And useful! And delicious. Mmm . . . eggs.

MARJORIE: I don't like eggs.

WALT: Everyone likes eggs! They go into cake! You like cake, don't you?

MARJORIE: No.

WALT: No? What's wrong with you? Everyone likes cake.

MARJORIE: I'm allergic.

WALT: Oh. But you like chickens, right?

MAJORIE: They're OK.

WALT: A minute ago they were cute.

MAJORIE: A minute ago you weren't trying to get me to gather the eggs for you.

WALT: How did you know?

MARJORIE: Eggs aren't cute.

WALT: Sure they are!

MARJORIE: You're weird, Walt.

WALT: Takes one to know one.

MARJORIE: I guess so. So, are you gonna get those eggs or not?

WALT: Not.

MARJORIE: Don't you have to?

WALT: Well, yeah.

MARJORIE: So? Go ahead.

(WALT *takes a deep breath and puts one hand into the chicken coop. He feels around for an egg. After a second, he pulls his hand out quickly.*)

WALT: Ouch!

MARJORIE: What?

WALT: That chicken bit me!

MARJORIE: Chickens don't bite.

WALT: This one did!

MARJORIE: It pecked you.

WALT: No one told me about this!

MARJORIE: Now you know.

WALT: So how am I supposed to do this?

MARJORIE: You're supposed to be brave and just do it.

WALT: Well, duh. Of course I will.

MARJORIE: So?

WALT: So?

MARJORIE: What are you waiting for?

WALT: Nothin'.

MARJORIE: Go on then!

(WALT hesitates, then puts his hand back in the chicken coop.)

WALT: Got one! Ouch!

(WALT pulls his hand out of the chicken coop again.)

WALT: Ow, ow, ow, ow, ow! I hate stupid chickens!

MARJORIE: Don't say that. They'll hear you.

WALT: They can't understand me. They're *stupid*!

MARJORIE: Maybe they're pecking you because you're mean.

WALT: I broke an egg that time!

MARJORIE: The eggs are their babies.

WALT: No they're not.

MARJORIE: Yes, they are. Where do you think chicks come from?

WALT: Well . . . but they're not *really* chicks. At least not yet.

MARJORIE: Well, yes and no.

WALT: This calls for drastic measures. I'll be back.

MARJORIE: What are you gonna do?

WALT: You'll see.

MARJORIE: Bring me back some chocolate milk, would ya?

WALT: No way!

(WALT exits.)

MARJORIE: Sometimes I see why moms have to nag all the time. Why can't kids ever just do something just because you asked them to? Especially boys. I hope my mother never hears me say this! Then it would be nag, nag, nag all day long. But I'm a helpful person, aren't I, chickens? It's not fair that stupid boys are allowed to take your babies and scramble and eat them. It's wrong, isn't it? And I'm not just saying that because I'm allergic. I would say it anyway. (Beat.) You know, you are pretty cute. Cute enough. Who needs to be bunny cute? My baby sister's bunny cute and she's stupid. My mom likes her best though. She says she doesn't, but she does. You chickens are practical and sensible and smart . . . I'm not gonna let anyone take your babies away. Don't you worry!

Scene 2: Plan B

(WALT returns, wearing a helmet and oven mitts. He holds a fork and a spatula. Around the chicken coop, a crowd has gathered.)

VIOLET: What are you going to do, Walt?

WALT: Get some eggs from that chicken coop.

TY: You're a dork, Walt. Just reach in and get them.

WALT: These are not ordinary chickens.

EMILY: Sure they are.

MARJORIE: They peck.

JOE: So?

WALT: So, it hurts!

TY: I think you're the chicken, Walt.

WALT: Look at my wounds.

(WALT takes off his oven mitts and shows them his hands. VIOLET, TY, EMILY, and JOE gather around him. MARJORIE stands off to the side, bored.)

EMILY: Ew!

JOE: Man, those chickens are evil!

MARJORIE: No, they're not.

TY: Shut up, Marjorie.

EMILY: You shut up!

TY: Are you her mother?

EMILY: Maybe I am.

JOE: You're young.

EMILY: So?

VIOLET: Don't fight, you guys!

MARJORIE: Those chickens are trying to save their babies.

WALT: No, they're not, Marjorie.

VIOLET: What do you mean?

MARJORIE: Eggs are where chicken babies come from. When you take and eat those eggs, you're eating a chicken baby. It's wrong. I hope that the chickens peck your hands off, Walt.

JOE: How come chicken babies are so gooey then?

MARJORIE: So were you when you were just starting to grow, too.

VIOLET: Marjorie, are you serious? That is so sad.

MARJORIE: It is sad. You shouldn't eat eggs. No one thinks about what they really are. Don't do it, Walt. Don't get those eggs. Your mom won't be mad if you explain it to her. It's not fair. Think about the little chick that might hatch from that egg.

WALT: You never said that before. Why are you all of a sudden so concerned?

MARJORIE: I got to thinking about it. And I decided it's wrong.

WALT: You're just allergic.

TY: You're allergic? That's cheating.

EMILY: That doesn't make sense.

JOE: Sure it does. It would be one thing to give up eggs; it's another thing to not eat them in the first place.

TY: Right.

VIOLET: Boys! They just don't understand. This is a tiny, helpless chick we're talking about.

WALT: If this gets me out of gathering eggs, I'm all for it.

EMILY: Aren't eggs in a lot of things, though?

MARJORIE: Yes.

WALT: Oh, yeah. Cake.

JOE: I like cake.

TY: You'd have to give it up.

VIOLET: I don't know if I could do that.

MARJORIE: That's because you're weak.

TY: No, I'm not!

JOE: Speaking of weak, you gonna get those eggs or not, Waltie?

WALT: Don't call me Waltie!

TY: Get the eggs!

JOE: GET THE EGGS! GET THE EGGS!

VIOLET, EMILY, TY, JOE: GET THE EGGS! GET THE EGGS!

WALT: OK! OK! Here I go!

(*MARJORIE throws herself in front of the chicken coop.*)

MARJORIE: Noooooo! Stay away from the defenseless chicken babies! You leave them alone, you monsters! They are just trying to stay warm and alive. It's not fair. What if someone did that to you when you were a baby! Took you away from your mother, scrambled you, and *ate* you!

(*VIOLET, EMILY, TY, JOE, and WALT are disgusted.*)

MARJORIE: That's right! It's gross. And not nice. And what if someone poked your mother with a fork for trying to protect you? Wouldn't you be mad? And there you are, ready to attack the mother chickens for doing their job. You're a terrible person, Walt. You should be ashamed of yourself. Plus, you're greedy. All you care about is getting eggs so you can have cake. Would you *die* if you couldn't have cake? No! No, you wouldn't. You're a greedy, bad person. I'm ashamed to know you.

(*WALT lowers his fork.*)

MARJORIE: That's right, Walt. Step away from the chicken coop. Let these chickens live in peace and harmony! Let these chickens live!

WALT: Are you done now?

MARJORIE: Yes. My job is done here.

EMILY: I love chicks. They're all yellow and fluffy.

VIOLET: So cute! You're so right, Marjorie.

EMILY: Let's get out of here.

(*MARJORIE, VIOLET, and EMILY exit. Beat.*)

JOE: So. Are you gonna get those eggs or are *you* the chicken?

WALT: Those chickens can't defeat me. I'm a warrior. Plus, my mom will kill me if I don't do this.

TY: Chicken! You're scared of your mom!

WALT: So I'm a chicken if I do this, and I'm a chicken if I don't.

TY: Yeah!

WALT: Everyone's scared of his mom. Don't pretend you're not. You have to be; otherwise the universe would be nuts. What if no one listened to his mother? We'd all be eating with our hands and burping at dinner and never taking baths. We'd be a completely disgusting society of slobs. Imagine the world if Ty told everyone what to do. Our tongues would be stuck to flagpoles, and we'd be throwing water balloons day and night. Let's face it; that would be pretty sick. I hate to say it, I really do, but a world without mothers would be a dark, scary place. Don't pretend like you don't believe me. You know it, too. I have to listen to my mother to keep the world from going crazy. So I guess I have to get eggs from the chicken coop after all.

JOE: Do it. I wanna see those chickens peck your hands off.

(WALT hands the fork and spatula to TY and JOE. With the oven mitts on, he sticks his hands in the chicken coop again.)

WALT: Ow! Ow! Ow! Ow!

JOE: Look at those chickens go!

TY: Come on, Walt! Get those eggs!

WALT: Ow! Ow! Ow! Ow!

(WALT finally pulls his hands out. He has four eggs.)

WALT: *(Yelling.)* Hey, Mom! I've got a bunch of eggs! Do

you think you could make a cake with them? *(Beat.)* Spinach quiche? Are you kidding?

JOE: Oh, man. You've been had.

TY: I like spinach. I'm like Popeye.

JOE: It didn't work.

TY: What?

JOE: The spinach.

TY: I'm stronger than you.

JOE: Are not!

TY: Prove it!

JOE: Let's go!

(JOE and TY exit, dropping the fork and spatula.)

WALT: Mom? Do I have to eat the quiche? *(Beat.)* Aw, man! I've got four. That's good enough, right? *(Long beat.)* Six more? Um, Mom? I think it's wrong to eat eggs. Did you know they're chicken babies?

TALK BACK!

1. Where do you stand on eating eggs and meat?

2. Is Walt a chicken or a warrior?

3. Are there boys' chores and girls' chores? Why or why not?

4. What do you think of Marjorie? Is she bossy or smart or both?

5. Should you have to do things you don't like to get things you want (in Walt's case, collect eggs to get cake)?

6. How can an actor show pain without actually feeling it?

THE BASEMENT

2F, 2M

WHO

FEMALES   MALES
  Mary   Mike
  O'Reilly, a leprechaun   Stan

WHERE Scene 1: A living room; Scene 2: A basement.

WHEN Present day.

🎭 Pay attention to the relationships between Mike, Mary, and Stan. Who's related to whom? Who's in charge? Who does your character like or dislike? How can you make O'Reilly seem like a leprechaun?

✍ In this play, I used a standard idea (what's in the basement?) and decided to twist it in a strange and unexpected way. Try the same thing. Write your own Scene 2 and have Mike, Mary, and Stan find something completely different in the basement.

Scene 1: The Dare

(MIKE and STAN enter the room.)

MIKE: I'm gonna beat you.

STAN: No way. I beat you the last three times.

MIKE: You got lucky.

STAN: You wish.

(MARY enters and pretends to turn on a TV.)

MIKE: What are you doing?

MARY: Watching TV.

STAN: Duh.

MIKE: Get out of here. We're playing video games in here.

MARY: No, you're not.

MIKE: That's because you're hogging the TV.

MARY: Be quiet, I'm trying to watch the TV.

STAN: Come on, Mary, get lost.

MARY: No way. You can't make me.

STAN: He can. Go on, Mike, get rid of her.

MIKE: Move it, Mary.

MARY: If you touch me, I'll tell Mom.

MIKE: You wouldn't dare.

MARY: Of course I would.

STAN: No, you wouldn't. You'll pay. Right, Mike?

MIKE: Right!

MARY: You don't scare me. Why don't you just go somewhere else?

STAN: *Because*, dummy, we're going to play video games.

MARY: No, you're not! Don't bully me, stupid Stan.

MIKE: Jeez, Mary, you always act like a baby.

MARY: You're always a bully!

MIKE: Come on, we can go to my room.

STAN: Not your room. It smells like socks.

MIKE: So does your room.

STAN: How about the basement?

MARY: We're not allowed in the basement.

STAN: Why not?

MIKE: I don't know. Dad just said we're never allowed to go down there.

STAN: What's down there?

MIKE: Dunno.

MARY: We're just not allowed. So you can't go down there.

STAN: I think we should. There's got to be something really good down there.

MARY: Like what?

STAN: I don't know, but we're going to find out—right, Mike?

MIKE: Well, maybe we should just go to my room. We could play a board game.

STAN: I hate board games. They're what your parents make you play when they don't want you to do something cool. It's like punishment.

MARY: I like board games. Especially Clue.

MIKE: You cheat at Clue.

MARY: I do not! I'm just smart.

STAN: Clue is for dorks.

MARY: So I bet you like it.

STAN: Ha, ha, ha. Very funny.

MIKE: Let's go play basketball.

STAN: No way. We already had gym class today.

MARY: Maybe you *should* go to the basement.

MIKE: You just want to have the TV to yourself.

MARY: Go to the basement, Mike. I dare you.

STAN: Maybe *you* should go to the basement.

MARY: Maybe not. Are you scared?

STAN: No.

MARY: So go to the basement.

STAN: Maybe I will.

MIKE: My dad's gonna get mad at you, just so you know.

STAN: Do you do everything your dad says?

MARY: Yes.

MIKE: No, I don't.

MARY: Yes, you do.

MIKE: No, I don't!

MARY: Yes, you do.

MIKE: I do whatever I want. I don't sit around and obey orders. I'm not a robot. *You* are, Mary. Always a Goody Two-shoes. Not me. I'm a rebel. So if I want to go into the basement, I go into the basement. I don't care what Dad or anyone says. Know what? I bet I probably *can* go into the basement. Know why? Because Dad likes me best, Mary. So you can just sit up here and watch your stupid TV show like a baby. *(Beat.)* Don't get all teary, Mary. You're always crying. I swear that you're only pretending most of the time to get attention. It's not going to work. You're just going to have to grow up. And you're going to have to accept that I'm the boss here, not you. I'm older and wiser. I get to do things first. So I'm going to the basement with Stan. And we're going to have fun. And Dad will not get mad at me because I'm the favorite. So you have a really good time up here by yourself.

MARY: I want to go to the basement, too!

STAN: Well, you can't. You heard him. You have to stay up here.

MARY: You're stupid, Stan. You can't tell me what to do.

STAN: Can and did.

MARY: Mike!

MIKE: Uh, Stan? Don't tell Mary what to do. That's my job.

STAN: Whatever.

MIKE: So, let's go, I guess.

STAN: What do you think is down there?

MIKE: Don't know.

STAN: What could be so bad?

MARY: You're a chicken, Stan.

STAN: I am the least chicken person you'll ever meet. I'll take any dare. Just ask Mike. One time I kissed Susie "Monkeyface" Benefisi on a dare. It was gross, but I did it. Another time, I touched Mrs. Doppler's butt. I pretended I tripped and had to get my balance. That was seriously gross. And *another* time, I climbed the highest tree at school and jumped off when I got to the top. I broke my leg. It was awesome. Oh, and I licked Becky Fernhauer's locker when she was sick with chicken pox and told Mr. Tolbert his fly was down when it wasn't. I'm the bravest kid you know. So going down to your dumb old basement is no big deal. What could be so bad? It's probably just filled with power tools your dad doesn't want you to touch. Big deal. It's not like you could have demons or monsters down there waiting to grab your legs and eat your face off. Demons don't even work like that. They'd probably just freeze you, so you couldn't fight, then eat your face off. They wouldn't want a struggle. So where's the basement?

MIKE: Maybe this isn't a good idea. Maybe we should play basketball.

MARY: Monsters are going to eat your faces off.

MIKE: No, they won't! That's just silly.

MARY: Go play in the basement, Mike, if you're so brave.

MIKE: Let's go, Stan.

STAN: See ya later, little baby.

MARY: I am not a baby! If demons eat your faces off, I'm not even gonna call the police!

STAN: We don't need the police. Me and Mike can defeat demons.

MARY: Can not!

MIKE: Can too!

STAN: See ya, shrimp.

Scene 2: The Discovery

MIKE: My dad is going to kill me.

STAN: Maybe monsters will kill you first.

MIKE: Shut up, Stan.

STAN: Make me, Mike.

MIKE: I can't see a thing.

STAN: Where's the light?

MIKE: By the wall.

STAN: Duh. Which one?

MIKE: That one.

STAN: Which one? I can't see you point in the dark. What do you think is down here for real?

MIKE: I don't know. All I know is that my dad always says "Don't go down into the basement!"

STAN: So you never, ever did?

MIKE: Ow! You stepped on me. No, I never, ever did.

STAN: Didn't you ever want to come down here?

MIKE: Sort of.

STAN: But you were scared!

MIKE: No. Not exactly.

STAN: Found it!

(The lights go on.)

STAN: So this is the basement. Looks like a normal basement.

MIKE: Yeah. I wonder why we weren't allowed down here.

STAN: Not even a chain saw or anything. Pretty boring.

MIKE: Weird.

STAN: Maybe there's a dead body somewhere.

MIKE: There's not a dead body.

STAN: Maybe your dad killed someone and stashed the body down here.

MIKE: My dad didn't kill anyone.

STAN: Maybe he did.

MIKE: He didn't, OK?

STAN: Take it easy. I'm just saying there's got to be *some* reason he doesn't want you to come down here. Let's look around.

MIKE: OK.

(STAN and MIKE walk around, looking into boxes, etc.)

STAN: Junk.

MIKE: Books.

STAN: This one's empty.

MIKE: Old toys.

STAN: Any good ones?

MIKE: No.

STAN: Boring.

MIKE: Boring.

O'REILLY: *(Entering.)* I'll tell you what's boring.

STAN: *(Not looking at O'REILLY.)* What?

O'REILLY: You two!

(MIKE turns around to look at O'REILLY.)

MIKE: Stan?

STAN: What?

MIKE: Stan?

STAN: *(Turning around.)* What? *(To O'REILLY.)* What are you?

O'REILLY: What do you think I am?

MIKE: One of Mary's friends?

STAN: A troll?

O'REILLY: Thank you very much.

STAN: You're welcome.

O'REILLY: I'm a leprechaun, you pea-brains!

STAN: I bet my brain is bigger than your brain.

MIKE: Stan—

O'REILLY: *(Coming close to STAN.)* I bet it's not!

MIKE: Stan—

STAN: How much do you wanna bet?

MIKE: Stan—

O'REILLY: What do ya got?

STAN: Nothing.

O'REILLY: Then what's the use of betting, pea-brain!

STAN: Leprechauns are boys.

O'REILLY: How do you know?

STAN: Everyone knows.

O'REILLY: Don't ya think I'd know better than you, pea-brain, seeing as I'm a leprechaun?

MIKE: Stan—

STAN: What?

O'REILLY: Yeah, what?

MIKE: Um, hi.

O'REILLY: Hello. What are you doing in my home?

MIKE: Actually, this is my home.

O'REILLY: Actually, this is *my* home.

MIKE: No, see, I live here. Upstairs.

O'REILLY: Exactly. Upstairs. And I live down here.

STAN: Why?

O'REILLY: Because I do, pea-brain.

MIKE: Do you know my dad?

O'REILLY: Your dad? Big man? Brown hair?

MIKE: That's him.

O'REILLY: No.

STAN: But you said—

O'REILLY: I say a lot of things. Now get out of my house.

STAN: Or what?

MIKE: Stan!

O'REILLY: Or you don't want to know what.

STAN: Do you have a pot of gold?

O'REILLY: If I did, would I tell you?

(STAN *starts opening boxes madly, looking for the gold.*)

O'REILLY: Those are *my* things.

MIKE: Yeah, Stan, stop!

O'REILLY: Listen to your friend here.

STAN: Or what?

O'REILLY: Or I will go through all of your things.

STAN: Go ahead.

O'REILLY: Ah-ha! Look what I found!

(O'REILLY *pulls a pair of underpants with ducks on them out of STAN's pocket.*)

MIKE: What are those?

STAN: Hey!

(STAN *tries to take the underpants back from O'REILLY and fails.*)

O'REILLY: I believe these are Mr. Stan's ducky underpants.

MIKE: You wear underwear with—

STAN: Shut up!

O'REILLY: Maybe you should go home now, Stan.

MIKE: Does he have anything else?

STAN: No!

O'REILLY: Are you sure, Stan?

(Beat.)

STAN: Fine. We'll go.

MIKE: No, I wanna see!

STAN: Stop it! Stop humiliating me! It's not fair. You're a leprechaun; of course I'd be curious about your stuff. It's natural. I can't be blamed for being curious. It's *human*. People are like that. Maybe you can't understand that since you're a . . . what are you? A person? A creature? Whatever! Not a regular human being. So I can't really help that I want to know things. I'm going to be a scientist someday. I need to study things and figure them out. So I have every right to come to your home and check things out. Plus, this isn't *your* house; it's Mike's dad's house. You don't own it. So you can stop looking at me like that. If you do anything to me, I'll go get the police and you'll be arrested. You'll go to prison and everyone will be a lot bigger and a lot meaner than you. So . . . stop trying to scare me. You don't scare me! I'm not scared of anything! Especially you. So . . . you can stop looking at me now! You're not scaring me!

O'REILLY: Curious, huh? Going to call the police, huh? And tell them there's a leprechaun *looking* at you? Go ahead, pea-brain.

STAN: Stop calling me that!

O'REILLY: Go home, Stan.

STAN: No!

O'REILLY: You're in love with Snow White.

STAN: No, I'm not!

O'REILLY: You kiss the poster in your room every night before you go to sleep!

STAN: No, I don't!

MIKE: Stan! That is sick!

STAN: It's not true! Listen, this is not cool. This is boring! Let's go play basketball. You're going to get in trouble if we stay down here, Mike. I don't want to get you in trouble.

O'REILLY: Now Stan is a good boy? Give me a break. I don't know why you think you can do whatever you want. You think just because you're human you're stronger than me. You're not! Hear that, little boy? You just pretend to have courage, Stan. I know what you really think. I know what you really feel.

You are only tough when you're the oldest and the biggest person in the room. But it's all a lie. When you're faced with something or someone bigger than you, you just crumble. Typical human! You step on a spider but you use a gun to face a bear. Courage is not having all the odds on your side. Courage is not kissing a girl you already like and you know likes you, too.

STAN: I do not like Susie Benefisi! And that's not my underwear! That is my baby brother's underwear. I guess my mom made a mistake when she put it away. I would never wear something with ducks on it, Mike. Let's just go now, Mike. This is seriously uncool.

O'REILLY: Good riddance.

MIKE: My dad will be home soon, I guess.

O'REILLY: And don't even think of coming back. You humans, besides being curious and weak, are also very pea-brained and silly. You all have a lot of secrets you don't want people to know. Think about that before you consider coming to the basement again! Everyone has things they don't want people to know or see. When something is forbidden, there is always a reason. Isn't that true, Stan?

STAN: Yeah. Sure. I guess.

O'REILLY: Would you like your underpants back?

STAN: They're not mine! So you can keep them. Whatever.

O'REILLY: Then I suggest you disappear.

STAN: Right! Let's go!

(STAN runs out.)

MIKE: So, sorry, I guess. I don't . . . We didn't mean . . . I hope you don't . . .

O'REILLY: Go away.

MIKE: OK. Bye!

(MIKE exits.)

O'REILLY: Ah, another pair of underwear for my collection! What would I do without curious children?

TALK BACK!

1. Is Stan a bully?

2. Is O'Reilly a bully?

3. Where do you stand on snooping?

4. Is O'Reilly justified in humiliating Stan?

5. What would you do if you found a pot of gold?

6. How would you react if you saw a leprechaun?

7. Do you think Mike's father knows about O'Reilly?

8. Why is O'Reilly there?

9. Is Stan right about curiosity being a natural human trait?

10. Should curiosity be encouraged or discouraged?

TREASURE!

5F, 5M

WHO

FEMALES	MALES
Amy	Angus
Jalinda	Giuseppe
Maddy	Horace
Nina	Roger
Ruby	Stanley

WHERE Scene 1: A desert island; Scene 2: At sea.

WHEN Daytime, over the course of two days. When pirates ruled the seas.

🎭 Try using a different voice or accent and moving in a different way. Most of the characters are pretty unusual, so you can have a lot of fun with it!

✎ This play is based on—you guessed it—the pirate genre. (A genre is a piece of writing that fits into a typical category like science fiction or romance.) Write your own pirate tale.

Scene 1: Treasure?

STANLEY: Here it is. X marks the spot.

NINA: Are you sure? Because I think we're two paces off.

STANLEY: Are you questioning me?

NINA: Yes.

STANLEY: Are you calling me stupid? I think I know how to read a treasure map!

NINA: We'll see about that—Maddy, start digging!

(*MADDY pokes the ground with a shovel.*)

MADDY: It's not here. Nothing but sand. Unless . . . Do you think sand is the treasure?

ANGUS: Ya big ninny! How could sand be a treasure? It's everywhere?

NINA: Maddy, take two steps to your left.

(*MADDY takes two steps forward.*)

STANLEY: To the left! To the left!

(*MADDY hesitantly takes one step backward and one step to the right.*)

STANLEY: Left! Left! That way! (*Points to the left.*)

(*MADDY takes four steps to the left.*)

STANLEY: No, no!

ROGER: Calm down. Maddy can't help it if she's lived her whole life pirating. Take one step behind you, and one step to the starboard side.

(MADDY takes one step back and one step to the right.)

NINA: Perfect! Don't move. Now dig.

(MADDY is not moving.)

STANLEY: Dig! Dig!

MADDY: She said not to move!

(GIUSEPPE pushes MADDY aside and takes the shovel.)

GIUSEPPE: I'll do it!

STANLEY: Wait! What if there's something horrible inside, like snakes?

GIUSEPPE: Don't be a wee girlie, Stanley!

NINA: Excuse me! I'm a girl!

ROGER: I'm sure he didn't mean that.

GIUSEPPE: Mean what?

NINA: Just dig!

(GIUSEPPE digs and finds the treasure chest.)

GIUSEPPE: Treasure!

STANLEY: Open it!

ANGUS: Hurry up!

ROGER: Stay calm, everyone.

NINA: Just be careful, Giuseppe.

   (GIUSEPPE slowly opens the treasure chest.)

STANLEY: Aaah! Snakes!

GIUSEPPE: No, it's . . .

ANGUS: Argh! Nothing!

ROGER: No, it's a map.

MADDY: Is it made of solid gold?

ROGER: I don't think so.

MADDY: So how is it a treasure?

ANGUS: It's not! Stupid treasure chest! I hate pirating!

NINA: Wait, wait, wait! It's a treasure map.

ROGER: Another one?

STANLEY: How do we know that this map won't lead us
   to another map, which leads us to another map, which
   leads us to another map . . . and we never find the actual treasure?

NINA: It might just be a joke.

MADDY: I don't get it.

ANGUS: Because it ain't funny! Why, I'll tear this map-maker apart if I ever find him!

ROGER: But what if *this* is the map that finally brings us to an *actual* treasure, filled with gold doubloons and red rubies and potato chips?

MADDY: What are potato chips?

NINA: They haven't been invented yet.

MADDY: Well, I know I'm not the clever one here, but it seems like all we do is look for things that we can't find, like treasure or islands. And if we actually *do* find something, it's not at all the way we think it will be. Remember when we found that exotic island with all the palm trees and coconuts? It seemed so nice there. The people were all so friendly! Pirate Bob was with us then. Pirate Bob was great, so chubby and cheerful. I liked Pirate Bob. I was so excited to have a meal that wasn't stale biscuits and salted pork. And there were so many new, wonderful foods there—brightly colored fruits, chocolate . . . I don't know why with all those delicious things, the natives would need to eat Pirate Bob. He *was* juicy and succulent, but I wasn't convinced it was necessary. I would have settled for a nice plate of monkey, personally. Maybe I'm not meant to be a pirate after all.

GIUSEPPE: Maddy, you can't give in. You must be brave and courageous and sneaky! It's the way of the pirate!

ROGER: Maddy, if you come along to our next adventure, we'll let you wear the eye patch.

MADDY: Really?

ROGER: We might sing a sea shanty or two!

MADDY: I love to sing!

ROGER: And I think we still have a pineapple from Cannibal Island.

MADDY: Can we put it on the salted pork?

ROGER: You bet!

STANLEY: Hurry up, then! Let's get in the boat. It's treasure for sure this time. I can feel it in my bones.

(The PIRATES climb onboard their boat.)

ANGUS: *(Singing to the tune of* "The Farmer in the Dell.") A-piratin' we go/ A-piratin' we go/ Hi-ho a-derry-o/ A-piratin' we go.

STANLEY: Quiet! I hear something.

RUBY: *(Offstage, screaming.)* GO AWAY! I HATE YOU!

STANLEY: It's beautiful!

ROGER: I'm in love.

ANGUS: She's mine!

MADDY: Mommy?

GIUSEPPE: We're changing course!

NINA: What? Wait. We're looking for treasure.

STANLEY: We're setting a course for love.

NINA: Have you all gone crazy?

(The boat shakes as the PIRATES crash against some rocks. RUBY appears.)

RUBY: Not again. This happens all the time.

NINA: They've all gone crazy.

RUBY: It's my voice. It attracts men and makes them go loopy.

ROGER: You're pretty.

RUBY: Yeah, yeah, yeah. You have the most beautiful voice, you have to marry me, blah, blah, blah. This happens every day. It's very boring. Thank goodness the last guy finally died of scurvy. I never thought I'd get rid of him.

NINA: You're a siren?

RUBY: It's a curse.

STANLEY: You have the most beautiful voice!

ANGUS: Marry me!

ROGER: Look! I've got an eye patch!

MADDY: Hey, that's mine now!

NINA: Listen, is there anything you can do to get us back on course? We're looking for treasure.

RUBY: Who isn't?

NINA: Can you be a little understanding?

RUBY: I'm just trying to live a quiet, peaceful life here. Really. I don't want to take over the world. I don't want the adoration of others. Sounds pretty simple, doesn't it? Instead I get this: Pirates and sailors trying to get my attention, talking to me, giving me orders all day and night. "Go away with me, Ruby!" "Sing for me, Ruby!" It's quite tiresome. I suppose I could just shut my mouth forever to keep them away, but is that fair? Shouldn't I get to express myself like everyone else? If a girlfriend comes by to chat and get a bite to eat, should I ignore her? Not that any friends come to visit me. I don't have friends. Girls hate me. I can't help that boys like me. If I could change things I would! I get very lonely. Being a siren is not all it's cracked up to be.

NINA: I can understand that.

RUBY: You can?

NINA: I feel sorry for you. It must be hard.

RUBY: It is!

NINA: Hey, I've got an idea. Tell the boys to go below deck and put some banana peels in their ears.

RUBY: Boys, go stuff banana peels in your ears.

MADDY: Hey, where's everybody going?

(STANLEY, ANGUS, ROGER, and GIUSEPPE disappear from sight and return soon after with "banana peels" in their ears.)

NINA: Tell them something else.

RUBY: What?

NINA: Anything!

RUBY: Boys, scratch your butts.

(MADDY, STANLEY, ANGUS, ROGER, and GIUSEPPE scratch their butts.)

NINA: Maddy, what are you doing that for?

MADDY: I itch.

NINA: Good point. They do that anyway. Say something else, siren.

RUBY: Hop on one foot.

(MADDY, STANLEY, ANGUS, ROGER, and GIUSEPPE stand still.)

NINA: It worked! Here's the trick. You need to tell them to stuff banana peels in their ears whenever you want to have a normal conversation.

RUBY: I guess that could work.

NINA: But first we need you to tell them to fix the ship and get back to finding the treasure. Hey, would you like to come along?

MADDY: Yeah!

RUBY: Well, OK. I've been wanting salted pork and stale biscuits for a while now.

NINA: Let's get to work! We're going to find treasure at last!

Scene 2: Quest

ROGER: *(Singing.)* Yo ho ho and a bottle of rum.

MADDY: That's a good one.

GIUSEPPE: It's good to be back at sea.

RUBY: I'll say.

ANGUS: I was gonna say it's good to be at sea, too!

STANLEY: I was gonna say it first, before anyone else said it!

ROGER: *(Trying to impress RUBY, too.)* I haven't got a single boil on my bottom!

(HORACE slowly, calmly enters.)

NINA: OK, OK! That's very, um, impressive, but let's get back to finding treasure. According to the map, we're getting close to—

(The ship rocks and there's a crash when HORACE bumps into the ship.)

ROGER: What was that?

GIUSEPPE: I don't see anything!

RUBY: Someone check it out!

STANLEY: Yeah, someone check that out!

ANGUS: Definitely! Just as soon as I . . .

MADDY: Um, I gotta go do something pirate-y.

GIUSEPPE: OK! Maddy, just stay where you are, ya liar. I'll do it!

(GIUSEPPE takes a deep breath to gain courage and looks over the side of the boat. He raises his head quickly and looks shocked.)

ROGER: What is it?

ANGUS: Speak up, Giuseppe!

GIUSEPPE: You guys are not gonna like this.

RUBY: Tell us!

GIUSEPPE: It's a kinda big, sorta—

ANGUS: Say it!

GIUSEPPE: —sea monster!

STANLEY: Aaah! Does it . . . look like a snake?

GIUSEPPE: A wee bit.

STANLEY: We're going to die.

NINA: Calm down. One of us just needs to assess the situation carefully, and we'll find a way out.

MADDY: No, we won't. We'll never get out. We're gonna die here!

ROGER: I once read a story about a great big monster.

It didn't have a happy ending. Not for the sailors, anyway.

GIUSEPPE: But we're pirates!

ANGUS: Right! We're much meaner than sailors.

STANLEY: So who's going down to check it out?

(The PIRATES all try to look busy, scratching their heads and looking at their feet, etc.)

RUBY: Fine! I'll do it!

(RUBY carefully and fearfully exits the ship and goes to see HORACE.)

RUBY: I mean you no harm. And if you're hungry, we have some salted pork on the ship. I'm pretty sure that I'd taste pretty terrible, so don't get any ideas, please—

HORACE: Gee whiz, I'm really sorry about that. I bump into stuff a lot.

RUBY: Uhhh—

HORACE: You have a pretty voice.

RUBY: Uhh—

HORACE: You seem like a nice lady.

RUBY: Uhhh—

HORACE: Oh, gee. You're scared, aren't you? It's because I'm a monster, isn't it? This happens all the time. I don't really know why. I was raised to be quite polite, a really nice monster. But no one seems to see the difference. All they see is MONSTER. There are good and bad monsters, you know. People think that we're all-powerful, too. But my gills hurt when I get splinters, just like yours do.

RUBY: I don't have gills—

HORACE: It's scary when people try to hurt you all the time, just because you look different. I mean, is this fearsome? *(HORACE does a little tap dancing.)*

RUBY: Aaah! Go away!

HORACE: Wait! What was so scary about that? I mean, I know I could use a few lessons, but . . . Listen, how about I just go away now? I'll just leave you alone and you leave me alone and we'll all live happily ever after. What do you think? I'm really sorry about bumping into your ship, and I'll try to look where I'm going in the future.

RUBY: Well . . .

HORACE: Please?

RUBY: You're very polite, aren't you?

HORACE: Of course. Manners are important.

RUBY: Wait a second. When I told you to go away, you didn't.

HORACE: Well, I didn't mean to be rude. I wanted to explain myself to you. I'm very misunderstood.

RUBY: You didn't listen to me. *(Beat.)* That's great!

HORACE: It is?

RUBY: Definitely! How are you at finding treasure?

HORACE: Pretty terrific. I bought myself a vacation cave in the Caspian Sea with some treasure doubloons.

RUBY: Fantastic! Hey, everyone, we're setting sail for treasure again!

PIRATES: Yippee!

RUBY: And the sea monster here is coming with us!

PIRATES: Yip—What?

HORACE: My name is Horace. Pleased to meet you.

RUBY: He's really quite nice. Let's set sail!

(ROGER, STANLEY, ANGUS, GIUSEPPE, and MADDY follow orders and get to work.)

NINA: Are you sure this is a good idea? He *is* a monster.

RUBY: It will be fine.

HORACE: Um, I can hear you, you know.

NINA: Horace, any idea where we are now?

ANGUS: We're lost! You had the map.

(ANGUS starts throttling ROGER.)

ROGER: *(Reaching in his pocket.)* It's here! It's here! Calm down, mate!

NINA: Let's ask for directions.

STANLEY: We don't need directions.

RUBY: Boys, thrust banana peels in your ears.

(ROGER, STANLEY, ANGUS, and GIUSEPPE put banana peels in their ears.)

NINA: Thanks. Now we can find out where we are. *(To HORACE.)* I don't suppose you know?

MADDY: I think we're at sea.

HORACE: I'm afraid I haven't a clue. I've been floating aimlessly for several days now. I'm on vacation, you see.

ROGER: That's quite understandable. *(Beat.)* My banana peels fell out.

(AMY and JALINDA enter.)

NINA: It's OK. We may be able to use you. I see some mermaids. *(To RUBY.)* Roger speaks mermaid.

RUBY: Ask them where we are, Roger.

AMY: Oh my God, it's pirates!

JALINDA: Get out! You are so right.

AMY: I know! Aren't I awesome?

JALINDA: Totally.

AMY: You're awesome, too, Jalinda!

JALINDA: Thanks, Amy. You're the best.

AMY: No, you're the best!

JALINDA: No—

ROGER: Excuse me, ladies.

AMY: Oh my God, he's talking to us!

JALINDA: That is totally crazy.

   (NINA *nudges* ROGER.)

ROGER: Can you, um, awesome ladies tell us where we are?

AMY: I guess.

JALINDA: Potentially.

ROGER: Oh my God, we would so, so appreciate it.

AMY: Really?

JALINDA: Oh my God!

AMY: He's totally cute.

JALINDA: And charming, for a pirate.

ROGER: We're trying to get to Devil's Cavern. Totally.

AMY: Ew!

JALINDA: There's no shopping there!

ROGER: Well, we're not going to shop.

AMY: Have it your way.

JALINDA: *(Points.)* It's right there.

ROGER: Thank you, ladies.

(*ROGER turns the ship in that direction.*)

AMY: That was totally weird.

JALINDA: You know it.

(*AMY and JALINDA exit.*)

STANLEY: Land ho!

(*STANLEY, GIUSEPPE, and ANGUS remove the banana peels from their ears.*)

MADDY: Treasure!

ANGUS: It better be or I'll . . .

HORACE: I say, why are you always so angry, friend?

ANGUS: No one's ever asked me that.

HORACE: I'm listening.

ANGUS: Well, I guess it all started when I was a wee, tiny pirate. The first time I went out to sea, I got my first taste of unsalted pork and fresh biscuits.

Ever since then, I've been a little disappointed with seafarin' food. Have ya ever gotten just plain tired of somethin'? You've had it so many times ya don't even taste it no more? Well, it makes me sore. And angry. Every time I taste salt . . . Well, it brings out me less gentle qualities. And everythin' tastes of salt—the food, the water, the very air! Plus, it ain't good for me heart. The sodium in salt raises your blood pressure, don't ya know. People think pirating is dangerous because of the lootin', the adventurin', the fightin', and the plank walkin'. Pirating is actually dangerous for yer health. And if Angus is one thing, it's concerned about his health.

HORACE: My friend, perhaps you weren't meant to be a pirate.

ANGUS: Let me finish! Lastly, and perhaps worstly, I can't get an even suntan. *(Beat.)* I'm done now.

HORACE: That is a tragedy. When we get ashore, maybe you should consider staying a while.

ANGUS: You've got a mighty point.

HORACE: Yes, it's called a horn.

ANGUS: Argh.

GIUSEPPE: If we find treasure, we won't ever have to go pirating again! We can just relax with our booty.

MADDY: What if it's just another map?

NINA: Only one way to find out! Let's go, everyone.

(All come ashore and exit.)

TALK BACK!

1. What was it like to be a pirate in reality? What were the hardships they faced out at sea?

2. Do you sympathize with Ruby?

3. Has anyone ever judged you—positively or negatively—for the way you look? Why do you think so?

4. Do you think you could survive a life at sea? Why or why not?

5. Why did pork have to be salted?

6. How can an actor seem like a mermaid or a sea monster without an expensive costume?

7. What could you do to make it seem like the male pirates are stuffing banana peels in their ears?

BOOGIE-MAN

4F, 2M

WHO

FEMALES

Gillian

Harper

Jessica

Mother

MALES

Father

Patric

WHERE Scene 1: Jessica's bedroom; Scene 2: The kitchen.

WHEN Present day. Scene 1: Night; Scene 2: Morning.

Color your words. For example, how can you make the word "creepy" sound creepy?

Try writing your own play about one way a parent can embarrass a kid. Make the play center around the characters' relationships rather than a lot of action.

Scene 1: Scary

(It's dark. PATRIC holds a flashlight.)

PATRIC: *(In a scary voice.)* It was a dark and stormy night. No one was around for miles. The kids were abandoned. Alone. The chaperones were lying dead at their feet. The silence was deafening. Then, a sound was heard in the distance.

(Suddenly, MOTHER enters. JESSICA, HARPER, and GILLIAN scream.)

MOTHER: That's enough. It's time for all of you to go to bed. Patric, off to your room.

PATRIC: At least let me finish my story.

MOTHER: I think you've done enough. OK, girls, into bed!

JESSICA: Mom, we're not tired.

GILLIAN: I promise I won't scream again.

MOTHER: Come on, let's go. Your parents won't be very happy with me if I return two exhausted girls to them tomorrow morning.

HARPER: I don't think I can sleep now.

GILLIAN: Don't be a baby, Harper.

HARPER: I can't help it!

PATRIC: Ha, ha, gotcha!

MOTHER: Harper, I don't know what stories Patric was telling you, but I assure you, you are totally safe here tonight. Now go to sleep. Patric, let's go.

(Reluctantly, the GIRLS get into their sleeping bags and PATRIC exits the room. MOTHER exits as they settle down.)

HARPER: I can't help it. I'm scared.

GILLIAN: I'm not. It's all fake.

JESSICA: You're scared, too. Don't lie, Gillian.

GILLIAN: No way. In fact, I'll finish Patric's story.

HARPER: That's OK. You don't have to.

JESSICA: Go on, then. You'd better be good.

GILLIAN: OK. The sound from the distance was coming closer and closer. The kids yelled out, "Is anyone there?" There was no answer. Just the sound of breathing and a final moan of pain from Mr. Lanker, lying dead at their feet.

JESSICA: If Mr. Lanker is dead, how can he make noise?

GILLIAN: Shut up, Jessica. Lying *almost* dead at their feet, OK? The kids tried to figure out what to do as the figure came closer and closer and closer. They didn't have anything they could use as a weapon except the pocket knife the killer used to tear Mr. Lanker to shreds.

HARPER: Can you kill someone with a pocketknife? Aren't they really small?

JESSICA: If you bleed enough, I guess you can die from anything.

GILLIAN: Be quiet! As I was saying . . . The killer had carved the six times table on Mr. Lanker's chest. Suddenly, Harper felt something touch her sleeve—

HARPER: Hey! Why is she called Harper? Not fair!

JESSICA: Because she is! Just be quiet!

GILLIAN: Harper said, "Is that you MaryAnn?" MaryAnn said, "I'm way over here trying to get a signal on my cell phone." "Well, then," Harper said, "Who's pulling at my sleeve?" No one answered. Total silence. Then—

(PATRIC *bursts into the room roaring menacingly. The girls scream.*

PATRIC: Ha, ha, ha. I so got you.

GILLIAN: Only because I was telling an excellent story.

HARPER: It was OK. Even I wasn't so scared.

GILLIAN: Liar! You were about to wet your pants.

HARPER: Was not!

(*MOTHER enters.*)

MOTHER: I thought I told all of you to go to bed.

JESSICA: Mom, Patric keeps bothering us.

MOTHER: Patric, what did I tell you?

PATRIC: I just wanted to finish my story. Can't I, Mom? It will only take one more minute.

HARPER: I think I need to know how it ends. But change the girl's name to something else!

GILLIAN: No, she's Harper.

HARPER: Stop!

MOTHER: Be nice, girls.

JESSICA: Please, Mom, can Patric finish his story?

MOTHER: I thought you wanted him to leave you alone.

JESSICA: I do, but . . . we just want to know the end. Then we want him to go away.

MOTHER: Well . . . One more minute, Patric. No more.

PATRIC: OK, Mom.

(MOTHER exits.)

PATRIC: OK. Hold onto your hats; this is gonna be good.

JESSICA: Just get on with it.

GILLIAN: Wait! So this girl Harper—

HARPER: MaryAnn! Call her MaryAnn!

GILLIAN: She feels something touching her sleeve, and it's not one of the other kids. And the math teacher, Mr. Lanker, is dead at their feet.

JESSICA: With the six times table carved into him.

PATRIC: That's good. Nice touch.

GILLIAN: Thank you.

PATRIC: OK. So, Harper—

HARPER: MaryAnn!

PATRIC: Harper feels something cold and clammy, almost metallic touch her arm. It's a hot, dry night in the desert, so the coldness gives her a chill. She moves away, closer to the group. Or at least she tries to. After one tiny step, she finds she can't move any further. Her clothes are caught on something! There are no trees, so she hasn't gotten caught on any branches. And though it's dark, she can make out the forms of her friends in front of her. Should she turn around? Should she rip her clothes and try to get free? Harper's breathing gets quicker as she tries to decide what to do. Just then she hears a voice. "Tell me your six times table," he hisses, in a quiet, menacing voice. Harper's throat is dry with fear. She begins, "Six times one is six, six times two is—"

(FATHER bursts into the room, making the KIDS jump.)

FATHER: Wooo! You kids are up late! Mom said she wanted you in bed now. Let's get moving!

(FATHER turns up the lights. He is wearing 1970s disco clothes—gold chains, tight pants, etc. The KIDS are stunned into silence.)

JESSICA: Dad, you promised not to come to my party!

FATHER: Come on, munchkin, give your old man a break! I just checked in to see how you were doing. Besides, I was always cool in school. All the kids liked me. I had the best moves in town. Very popular with the ladies, if you can believe it. I'm an old man now, but I've still got my moves.

(FATHER starts disco dancing wildly. The KIDS all scream in horror.)

JESSICA: Dad, stop!

PATRIC: Please, I'm begging you!

GILLIAN: It's horrible!

HARPER: I'm scared!

FATHER: It's not a party without dancing, right? Who wants to dance with me? Jessica?

JESSICA: No way, Dad!

FATHER: Ah, when Jessica was a little girl, we'd boogie every night after dinner.

JESSICA: Shut up, Dad!

FATHER: Patric there had some mean moves, too. He could spin just like Michael Jackson.

PATRIC: That information does not leave this room!

FATHER: Come on, let's dance!

(FATHER pulls HARPER onto her feet.)

FATHER: Woo! Yeah!

(HARPER stands totally still as FATHER dances around her.)

FATHER: Come on, show me some dance moves, Harper! Don't be shy!

HARPER: I—I—

FATHER: Gillian, you're the bold one here. I bet you've got some mean moves you do at the school dances.

(FATHER approaches GILLIAN who screams and buries herself in her sleeping bag. MOTHER enters.)

MOTHER: OK, that's it. Enough excitement for one night. Everyone, get in bed and go to sleep.

FATHER: The party was just getting started!

MOTHER: Gerry, these kids need to get some sleep.

FATHER: Don't be uncool and heavy, Helen. We're having fun. Right, kids?

MOTHER: Come on, Gerry. We can have a party of our own downstairs.

FATHER: You'll boogie with me, baby?

MOTHER: Sure.

FATHER: OK! You kids get in bed. Sleep well!

(FATHER dances out of the room.)

JESSICA: Mom, you said he wouldn't come!

MOTHER: Now, Jessica, he's your father. He just meant well.

PATRIC: His "moves" are a little old, Mom.

MOTHER: Patric, don't speak that way about your father!

PATRIC: I was just telling the truth, Mom. You like it when I tell the truth.

MOTHER: Enough! I've heard enough from you. Now get to your room, Patric.

(PATRIC exits.)

MOTHER: I expect you girls to settle down and get to sleep. We'll have pancakes in the morning.

(MOTHER exits. Long silent beat.)

JESSICA: You guys, I'm so sorry. My dad is a total embarrassment.

GILLIAN: No! All dads are kinda embarrassing. My dad calls everyone by weird nicknames. Most of them are food names like cupcake and cookie and stuff. I don't know what his deal is with that. Once I called him creampuff and he *liked* it! He thought it was cute. I thought it would get him to stop. Pumpkin, sugarplum—the list goes on and on. And it's bad enough he'd do it to me. He'd do it to you, too. He can't stop himself. He'll call anyone by a silly food name. He'll say it to waitresses and stuff. "I'll have an egg salad sandwich, tootsie pop, with a coke." And then they're like, "We don't have toot-sie pops." And I just wanna die. I swear. One time I called him banana cream pie. One time I called him brussel sprout casserole. He didn't care! You could call him spinach and hair milkshake, and he'd think you really thought he was swell. What's wrong with that man? So all dad's are weird, Jessica. Just in different ways.

JESSICA: Not like that.

HARPER: He seemed nice.

JESSICA: He is nice, he's just . . . Listen, he's a really nice guy and a good dad. He just doesn't know that it's the twenty-first century. It escaped him somehow. And we've tried buying him other clothes, but he won't wear them. And we've tried getting him not to dance, but he won't listen. He won a trophy in a disco contest on TV in 1978. You know how some guys win football games in high school, and it's, like, the most important thing in the world to them for the rest of their lives? Well, that's how disco danc-ing is for my dad. Actually, he was really good. For that kind of old-fashioned dancing. He could pick a girl up and hold her over his head and turn her around. And she wouldn't fall! And he'd put her down, and they'd spin. They'd spin so fast, almost like ice skaters. It was amazing. But, you know, lame. So he just keeps doing it. He doesn't know he's scary. I try to tell him, but . . .

HARPER: It's OK, Jessica.

JESSICA: I know, but . . . Sometimes I wish I had another dad.

GILLIAN: I'm tired. Let's get some sleep.

Scene 2: Cruel

(HARPER, GILLIAN, JESSICA, and PATRIC sit around the breakfast table.)

HARPER: I'm so glad it's morning. Everything always seems better in the morning.

GILLIAN: That's the real test, Patric, if you can be scary in the morning.

JESSICA: He's scary all the time.

GILLIAN: He's a brother. They can't help it.

(MOTHER enters.)

MOTHER: Good morning, kids. Did everyone settle down and get some sleep last night?

JESSICA: Yes, Mom.

MOTHER: How about you, Harper?

HARPER: Well, not really. I just kept thinking about that story with the girl and the man with the hook.

MOTHER: Patric, I told you not to tell that one.

PATRIC: That's a good one!

(FATHER enters.)

FATHER: Gooooood morning! I am digging this sunshine today!

(MOTHER, PATRIC, JESSICA, GILLIAN, and HARPER all go completely still and silent.)

FATHER: Why all the long faces? It's a groovy morning!

PATRIC: Dad, how many times do I have to tell you that no one unbuttons more than three buttons on a shirt?

FATHER: Son, you are one funny cat.

MOTHER: Honey, what can I get you for breakfast?

JESSICA: You guys should have breakfast out.

MOTHER: We have plenty of food here.

JESSICA: It would be good for you to go *out* together.

FATHER: Your mom's right. I'd like a nice, quiet breakfast at home with my family and my daughter's friends.

JESSICA: Daaad!

GILLIAN: I'm done with my breakfast. My parents will be wondering when I'm coming home. I'm, uh, supposed to clean the garage or something today.

FATHER: I wish I could get these kids to do that!

MOTHER: You're a very good daughter, Gillian.

GILLIAN: Thanks. So, I'll be going.

HARPER: Wait! Um, I should walk home with you. My parents don't like me to walk home alone.

FATHER: I could give you a ride home.

HARPER: That's OK. I can walk.

GILLIAN: So let's get going now.

HARPER: Bye! Thank you!

GILLIAN: Yeah, thanks for everything!

JESSICA: Bye, you guys!

(GILLIAN and HARPER exit. Beat.)

JESSICA: Thanks a lot, Dad.

FATHER: For what?

JESSICA: For completely embarrassing me in front of my friends!

FATHER: How did I do that?

JESSICA: With your stupid clothes and your dance moves! You're a total humiliation! You look like an idiot, Dad.

MOTHER: Jessica! That's enough!

JESSICA: What? It's true. No one wants to be around him. It's not 1978 anymore, Dad. Try living in the present day already!

PATRIC: Jess, calm down.

JESSICA: Easy for you to say! Your friends weren't here. So they'll still be talking to you in school on Monday.

FATHER: I was nice to your friends. I think you're being a little sensitive.

JESSICA: Maybe I am! But that's the way it is. I'll be a laughingstock in school forever, thanks to you! I wish I had a different father! I wish I lived in a different house! I wish you would disappear!

MOTHER: Jessica, that is enough! Go to your room!

FATHER: No, no, Judy. It's OK. Maybe she's right.

MOTHER: She's not right! She's being cruel and childish and insensitive.

FATHER: Well, maybe we should go out to breakfast after all, Judy. Let's go get some pancakes.

MOTHER: Fine. But you are not to leave the house all day, young lady! I want you to think about what you've done while we're gone. We will speak to you later!

(MOTHER and FATHER exit. Beat.)

PATRIC: Good job, moron.

JESSICA: What are you talking about? You should thank me.

PATRIC: For what?

JESSICA: For shocking Dad into living in this century.

PATRIC: Why would I thank you for that?

JESSICA: Because maybe now he won't be a total embarrassment to be around.

PATRIC: He's not so embarrassing.

JESSICA: Yes, he is!

PATRIC: Well, he is a little, but it's not like Mom's not embarrassing, too. She made me go out with her last week to buy new underwear. It was horrible.

JESSICA: Yeah, but that's just mom stuff. She *has* to buy you underwear. That's not the same.

PATRIC: Sure it is! Everyone's embarrassing in some way. Like you, for instance.

JESSICA: I'm not embarrassing!

PATRIC: Oh yes, you are.

JESSICA: Oh yeah? How!

PATRIC: You're annoying, you're a kid, you're a *girl* kid, you love the color pink, you call me Patty sometimes even though my name is *Patric*—

JESSICA: Mom calls you Patty—

PATRIC: —you *giggle* all the time, if I talk to a girl you say things like "Are you going to marry her, Patty?" in a really annoying voice, you leave these teen magazines around the house and tell my friends that they're mine . . . Should I keep going?

JESSICA: No.

PATRIC: And now you're pouting. Like I hurt your feelings. Don't you get it? You're such a dimwit, I swear. That's how it feels to be Dad. You're always picking at him. Telling what's wrong with him. He's just trying to be cool. He's not, but he's trying. That more than a lot of kids get.

JESSICA: I know, I know, he's not beating me or anything.

PATRIC: It's more than that. He's trying to be *nice*. He's trying to be a *dad*. Maybe he's not perfect. But you shouldn't be such a brat.

JESSICA: Like you never are.

PATRIC: I didn't say I was perfect. I'm not. But you shouldn't be so mean. Try to be a little mature.

JESSICA: Whatever.

(PATRIC exits. GILLIAN enters.)

GILLIAN: Hey!

JESSICA: Hey! Why are you here?

GILLIAN: I forgot my toothbrush.

JESSICA: Oh.

GILLIAN: I had a really good time yesterday. I swear I've never screamed so much in my life. Your dad is crazy!

JESSICA: Yeah, about that—

GILLIAN: Could he really pick up a lady and spin her over his head like a disco dancer?

JESSICA: Well, yeah—

GILLIAN: That is so awesome. I wish I could pick someone up over my head. I'd throw my little sister in the trash! Harper was saying on the way home how embarrassed she was about not knowing how to dance. I don't know how to dance either! No one ever taught me. And she was so scared going home by herself after those ghost stories! Oh, I gotta grab my toothbrush and get home. My dad is going to kill me if I don't clean the garage. I wish I didn't have to! I wish my dad were cool with the garage being a wreck like everyone else's is! Thanks so much for a really fun time, Jessica. I swear I almost wet my pants screaming and laughing! That's the mark of a really good party in my book. Your dad is excellent. Maybe you could teach us some boogie moves sometimes. It would be so funny to break those out at a school dance and be like, "We're cool. Don't you wish you could do this?" Well, see ya!

(GILLIAN starts to exit.)

JESSICA: Wait! You really had to go home to clean the garage?

GILLIAN: Yeah. Pretty stupid, right?

JESSICA: And Harper was really scared to walk home alone?

GILLIAN: Definitely! It was so funny. I made her jump a

couple of times on the way home, too. Well, I gotta run!

(GILLIAN exits. PATRIC enters.)

JESSICA: Patric, want to do something today? I'm grounded, I guess.

PATRIC: No way, little dweeb!

JESSICA: Please?

PATRIC: What do you want to do?

JESSICA: We could watch a movie.

PATRIC: We don't like the same movies. Face it, kid, we're different.

(PATRIC exits.)

JESSICA: Why is everyone so confusing?

TALK BACK!

1. Who's right about the father, Jessica or Patric?

2. Can you understand Jessica's point of view regarding her father?

3. Could Jessica handle the situation differently with her dad?

4. Do you think parents get their feelings hurt by kids?

5. What does being "adult" mean?

6. Is Gillian being honest or kind at the end?

7. Why do people like ghost stories?

ESP: EXTRA-SCARY PERCEPTION

9F, 9M

WHO

FEMALES	MALES
Colleen	Dad
Jennifer	Dean
Josie	Faber
Kelly	Howie
Lori	Joe
Lottie	Luke
Mom	Mark
Natalie	Peter
Teacher	Sullivan

WHERE Scene 1: At home; Scene 2: At school.

WHEN Present day.

One way to get into character is to decide your character's likes and dislikes, dreams and fears. Try it!

Write your own play about getting ESP. What's good and what's bad about being able to read other people's minds?

Scene 1: Strangeness

(MOM, DAD, COLLEEN, and DEAN are sitting and eating breakfast. LOTTIE rushes in suddenly and starts making her breakfast.)

LOTTIE: I know, I know, I'm late! Hurry up! You don't have to tell me. *(Beat.)* Mom! I do not do this all the time!

MOM: I didn't say anything.

LOTTIE: Yeah, right. *(Beat.)* You're right, Dad. There is too much drama in this house.

DAD: Huh?

LOTTIE: See, Mom, Dad likes me like I am. He doesn't want to change me all the time.

MOM: I like you how you are. I just wish you wouldn't be late in the morning. It ruins your whole day when you can't eat a proper breakfast.

LOTTIE: Oh, yeah. You're so great, Dean. Making it downstairs to breakfast ten minutes before me makes you so cool. Too bad no one likes you.

(At this moment, all stop bustling and freeze except DEAN and LOTTIE. DEAN stands and walks to the front of the stage.)

DEAN: I wish she wasn't so mean to me. I don't need to be reminded that I don't have as many friends as her. Can't I just get through breakfast without being reminded of my pathetic life? Would it be so much to

spend fifteen minutes without being made fun of? I get enough of that when I get to school. Thanks a lot, sis. You're great. You're so cool. No wonder you're popular in school. You're such a nice person.
(DEAN walks back to his seat and the scene returns to normal.)

LOTTIE: Dean, did I . . . hurt your feelings?

DEAN: Please. You wish.

LOTTIE: But . . . ?

DEAN: Shut up, weirdo.

LOTTIE: But . . . whatever.

(LOTTIE sits down with the rest of the family. Suddenly DAD stands and speaks, facing front.)

DAD: I hate this house. I can't stand this house. I feel trapped. Get me out of here!

(DAD sits down calmly.)

LOTTIE: Dad?

DAD: Yes, honey?

LOTTIE: Are you OK?

DAD: Certainly.

(Beat.)

LOTTIE: Are you sure?

DAD: Yes. *(Stands and faces front.)* Why do I have to explain myself all the time to this family? I bring in money so they can eat and have a roof over their heads, isn't that enough? *(Sits.)*

LOTTIE: Well, yeah, that's enough. I didn't mean to bother you.

DAD: What?

LOTTIE: I didn't mean to bother you. I was just trying to be nice. Even though Dean thinks I'm not nice, I was just trying to show that I'm a good daughter and I listen to you. You guys don't give me enough credit.

(COLLEEN, the baby, suddenly stands.)

COLLEEN: Milk! Milk!

MOM: Yes, honey. You want milky-wilky?

LOTTIE: Mom, you should speak to her like a person. She's a person.

MOM: I spoke to you this way.

LOTTIE: And I hated it.

(MOM faces front and steps forward.)

MOM: I can't believe this is the daughter I raised. What happened to the sweet little girl who liked to play on the swings and eat strawberry ice cream? How could I have raised such a brat?

(MOM goes to get COLLEEN her milk from the cupboard.)

LOTTIE: I am not a brat!

MOM: Well, yes you are. Or you're behaving like one today.

(DAD stands. The next several lines happen very quickly.)

DAD: I have to get out of here! You're all driving me crazy!

(DAD sits. MOM faces out.)

MOM: I wish I could have some peace and quiet and some nice, decent, well-behaved children for one day of my life!

(COLLEEN stands.)

COLLEEN: Milk!

(MOM brings COLLEEN her milk. COLLEEN and MOM sit. DEAN stands.)

DEAN: No one notices me. I am invisible! Mom loves the baby most, and Dad loves Lottie most, and then there's me. All alone. I hate everything!

(DEAN sits. LOTTIE stands.)

LOTTIE: Is this whole family going crazy?

MOM: What the problem now, Lottie? We're all just trying to enjoy a nice, quiet meal.

LOTTIE: **I don't know what you think is a nice, quiet meal, but this isn't it. Dad's screaming that he** wants to get out of the house, you're thinking I'm a horrible brat and you wish I wasn't alive, Dean's thinking I'm cruel and no one pays attention to him, Colleen keeps screaming for milk—

COLLEEN: Milk!

LOTTIE: This whole family is going crazy! Everyone keeps standing and sitting and saying the most awful things. You're scaring me! Really. This isn't right. I don't know why you're all acting this way all of a sudden. Today is the same as every other day. How come today everyone is so mean? Dad, I don't know why you want to get away from me so badly. I'm always nice to you. I can see if maybe Dean isn't so crazy about me, I am a little mean to him sometimes—

DEAN: Sometimes! More like all the time!

LOTTIE: —but I'm always nice to you! And Mom, it's your job to love me. How come you hate me so much? It's not allowed. I'm almost a teenager. I complain sometimes. So sue me! I hate all of you. You're all terrible. And I want to get out of this house, too. Unfortunately, I'm not old enough yet.

(Beat. LOTTIE sits.)

MOM: I never said I wish you were never born.

LOTTIE: Yes, you did. You said that you don't know how you raised such a brat and how I was such a nice little girl and I liked strawberry ice cream.

MOM: I didn't say that.

LOTTIE: Yes, you did.

DEAN: No, she didn't, nutcase.

(DAD stands.)

DAD: Everyone, will you please shut up! I want to enjoy a meal in silence!

(DAD sits.)

LOTTIE: Jeez, Dad, take it easy. You're going to have a heart attack or something.

DAD: I'm fine.

LOTTIE: You were just screaming.

DAD: No, I wasn't.

LOTTIE: Yes, you were. About how you want everyone to shut up so you can eat in silence.

DAD: I . . . *thought* that, but I didn't *say* it.

MOM: Lottie, you're scaring me a little. *(Beat.)* That thing about the ice cream, I *thought* that as well.

DEAN: Oh my God! *(Stands.)* Don't think bad thoughts! Don't think bad thoughts! *(Sits.)*

DAD: Do you think it's possible . . . ?

MOM: Can a person read minds?

DAD: What am I thinking now? *(Stands.)* Watermelons. *(Sits.)*

LOTTIE: Watermelons.

MOM: What about me? *(Stands.)* I've got to do the iron-ing, vacuuming, and wash Dean's underwear. *(Sits.)*

LOTTIE: You've got to vacuum, iron, and wash Dean's underwear.

DEAN: No fair!

COLLEEN: Cookies!

LOTTIE: *(Pointing to DEAN.)* No fair. *(Pointing to COLLEEN.)* She wants cookies.

DEAN: We both said those things out loud, dummy.

LOTTIE: I can't even tell anymore!

DEAN: ESP is not actually possible. Scientists have tested it. It's bogus. A certain amount of the time people guess things right by sheer luck. Especially when you know something about the person or the situation, which you totally know in this case since you're related to us. So guessing that Mom's think-ing about housework is a no-brainer. She's always saying she has too much to do. Plus, people can learn to read people's body language really well. That's what so-called psychics do. Dad is sitting with his arms folded. He could be stressed or want to get away. And psychics say general information. Anyone could do it. I could pretend to read your mind now, Lottie. You're probably thinking I'm a stupid dork.

LOTTIE: Lucky guess.

DEAN: See? Anyone can do it. You don't have powers. No one does. The only real power is knowledge. The mind is capable of incredible things. Like it can stop thinking conscious thoughts, clearing the mind—that's what Buddhist monks try to do—and continue involuntary thoughts that keep us breathing and stuff. So stop pretending to be psychic already. I don't know if you're just trying to get attention, but it's really weird, even for you.

LOTTIE: Why don't you demonstrate the clearing the mind stuff right now?

DEAN: Fine. I'll clear my mind right now.

(Beat. DEAN closes his eyes. Beat. DEAN stands suddenly.)

DEAN: Lindsey Lohan! *(Sits.)*

LOTTIE: Lindsey Lohan!

DEAN: No fair!

LOTTIE: I was right! And you have no chance with her.

DEAN: Duh. I know that.

DAD: She was right.

DEAN: Well . . . yeah.

DAD: You *can* read minds.

LOTTIE: I guess so.

DAD: We are all in really big trouble.

Scene 2: Freakville

LOTTIE: Don't be psychic. Don't be psychic. Don't be psychic. You don't want to read these people's minds! These people are animals. Shut them out. Or do I want to read their minds, find out their secrets? It could be interesting. I could blackmail them and get rich! Then again, do I really want to know if Howie secretly eats bugs or if Kelly hates me? No! But this is definitely real. This is definitely happening, right? I'm not crazy. Well, I am, but I'm not. I mean, I'm not making this up. If I made this up, it would be a lot more fun. This *is* supposed to be fun! I'm supposed to be able to use this information for my own evil purposes! People are supposed to think funny things, not sad, depressing stuff. And I've had just about enough of boring stuff. If I hear one more person think about what they're going to wear or eat for lunch, I'll scream! OK, classmates, dazzle me!

(SULLIVAN stands.)

SULLIVAN: Kelly smells like flowers.

(SULLIVAN sits.)

LOTTIE: Ugh!

(KELLY stands.)

KELLY: I hate this shirt. I can't believe my mom made me wear it. I look like a dork.

LOTTIE: You do look like a dork.

KELLY: I want to go home!

LOTTIE: You can't go home.

(KELLY sits slowly, looking scared. The TEACHER enters the room.)

TEACHER: Class, take out a pencil. We are having a test today.

(All students except LOTTIE stand and scream in unison, then sit. TEACHER passes out the tests.)

TEACHER: Eyes on your own paper. Start now.

(LUKE stands.)

LUKE: A, C, D, A, B, B, B. True. False. President Lincoln was shot in a theater. Jefferson Davis. Gettysburg.

(LUKE sits. During his speech, LOTTIE frantically circles and writes the answers he calls out.)

TEACHER: Time's up! Pass forward your tests.

(The STUDENTS pass up their tests. HOWIE stands.)

HOWIE: I totally failed. *(Sits. To LOTTIE.)* I totally failed.

LOTTIE: You're not very complicated are you, Howie?

HOWIE: Huh?

TEACHER: Quiet, please. Read from chapter eleven while I grade your tests.

(During the next section, the STUDENTS speak one right after the other, even overlapping their lines.)

LORI: *(Stands.)* Mark Gilbert is sooo cute.

HOWIE: *(Stands.)* This is boring.

NATALIE: *(Stands.)* I wish I were on TV.

PETER: *(Stands.)* I'm going to beat up Luke at lunch.

LUKE: *(Stands.)* "After Lincoln's death, Vice President Andrew Johnson . . ."

JENNIFER: *(Stands.)* Mark Gilbert is so cute.

MARK: *(Stands.)* I hope those two girls don't poke me all through lunch again.

JOE: *(Stands.)* It would be funny if I made a farting noise now.

FABER: *(Stands, sings.)* La la la la la.

JOSIE: *(Stands.)* How long 'til school's over? I'm starving!

LORI/JENNIFER: *(Stands.)* Mark Gilbert is *sooo* cute!

PETER: *(Stands.)* I hate Mark Gilbert. I'll beat him up at lunch.

JOE: *(Stands.)* How does that joke go about the three guys in the boat?

LUKE: *(Stands.)* . . . and the nation remained divided . . .

FABER: *(Stands, singing.)* La la la la la.

HOWIE: *(Stands.)* Boring, boring, boring.

NATALIE: *(Stands.)* At the Oscars I would wear a red dress.

FABER: *(Stands.)* La la la la la!

LOTTIE: Aaaaaah!

TEACHER: Lottie? What are you doing?

LOTTIE: Well . . . I . . .

(The bell rings and the STUDENTS exit in a hurry.)

TEACHER: Lottie and Luke, stay after class.

LOTTIE: I'm sorry about that. I got . . . overwhelmed.

TEACHER: Yes, well, I've asked you to stay after class for another reason.

LUKE: I'm already tutoring a lot of students. I don't think I could do any more and keep up my own work.

TEACHER: Luke, who killed Abraham Lincoln?

LUKE: John Wilkes Booth.

TEACHER: Lottie, describe General Lee?

LOTTIE: It's orange, has four wheels—

LUKE: She means the man, not the car!

TEACHER: That's enough, Luke. You can go now.

LUKE: OK.

(*LUKE exits.*)

TEACHER: Lottie, you cheated on this test.

LOTTIE: No, I didn't.

TEACHER: You answered all the questions *exactly* the same as Luke.

LOTTIE: Coincidence?

TEACHER: I don't think so.

LOTTIE: But we were sitting on opposite sides of the room.

TEACHER: True. I don't know how you cheated, but it's clear that you did.

LOTTIE: Well, I couldn't help it.

TEACHER: I'm going to help you out then.

LOTTIE: That's not going to be good, is it?

TEACHER: You're going to copy out the test questions and answers ten times.

LOTTIE: (*Speaking in unison with teacher.*) —copy out the test questions and answers ten times. No! I mean, don't you see? I couldn't help it!

TEACHER: Lottie, this isn't a joke. And when you're done with that, you can copy—

LOTTIE: —chapter eleven out of the textbook!?

TEACHER: The best thing for you to do right now is get to work and stop arguing.

LOTTIE: But—

TEACHER: *(Warningly.)* Lottie . . .

LOTTIE: I'm psychic! I can tell what other people are thinking.

TEACHER: Oh really? Then what am I thinking?

LOTTIE: You're thinking that you wish the cafeteria had tater tots today.

TEACHER: I think that every day. I probably told you that once.

LOTTIE: Now you're thinking you don't believe me.

TEACHER: Of course I don't believe you!

LOTTIE: Think of something totally different then!

TEACHER: Fine. Give me a minute.

(TEACHER takes a moment to think of something new.)

LOTTIE: Ew! What's that?

TEACHER: What's what?

LOTTIE: There's a picture, a painting of a man and it's all reddish and he's . . . I think his guts are being pulled out by a bird!

TEACHER: That's a famous painting.

LOTTIE: Don't tell me you still don't believe me.

TEACHER: Well . . . I guess I have no choice. That was very impressive.

LOTTIE: That's the first time you said I was impressive.

TEACHER: So how does this ability make you cheat?

LOTTIE: I can't stop hearing people's voices.

TEACHER: You can't block them out?

LOTTIE: I don't know. I don't think so. That's why I screamed before. Everyone was so noisy. Plus, Mark Gilbert is not that cute.

TEACHER: It seems to me that you can be selective. Why did you cheat off of Luke and not another student? How could you focus in on just his thoughts?

LOTTIE: They were the loudest?

TEACHER: Sorry, Lottie that theory doesn't work for me. If this is in fact true, this psychic thing, then I think you do have some control over it. So you can start writing out the test now. In an hour or so, you'll know more about history than even Luke does.

(TEACHER exits.)

LOTTIE: I hate this, I hate this, I hate this! I knew I should have asked the genie for another wish! But it seemed like such a good idea. But now I know my dad wants to get away from his family, my mom hates me, my brother hates me (well, I knew that), the bus driver didn't take a shower, and lots of girls think Mark Gilbert is cute . . . I can't even get away with cheating on tests! What's the use of having a superpower if you can't use it for fun? That's it! I don't want to be psychic anymore. "I wish I could not be psychic anymore!" Oh no! Why am I so impulsive? Why don't I think things through? Now I'm not special anymore. Now I have no powers. Now I can never go on TV and make lots of money guessing that people know someone whose name begins with the letter "D"—I was going to be rich and famous! Much richer and more famous than Natalie Greenberg. Now I'm nothing! Nothing! Nothing good ever happens to me. I'm doomed! I wish something good would happen to me! *(Beat.)* Oh no! I made another wish! That's it then. It's over. But I messed up! No fair! Do over!

(MARK enters.)

MARK: Oh, hi, Lottie.

LOTTIE: Hi.

MARK: What are you doing in here?

LOTTIE: I have to copy stuff out as punishment.

MARK: That's annoying.

LOTTIE: I know! What are you doing in here?

MARK: Jenn and Lori are just bugging me, so I had to get away, know what I mean?

LOTTIE: I guess so.

MARK: Yeah. So. You want me to help you with the copying?

LOTTIE: Our handwriting's different.

MARK: Well, if we both print . . .

LOTTIE: That's so nice.

MARK: No big deal.

LOTTIE: Seriously, you'd help me? Because you don't have to. I don't know if I'd help you.

MARK: It's OK. I don't mind. It's something to do.

LOTTIE: Wow. Thanks.

MARK: Lottie, how come you never poke me?

LOTTIE: What?

MARK: Most of the other girls do. It's like a sport with them. I don't know why they pick on me. It's annoying.

LOTTIE: They think you're cute.

MARK: Weird. Whatever.

(Beat.)

MARK: So I guess we're just friends, right?

LOTTIE: Right.

MARK: Oh. Great.

LOTTIE: I guess we should start writing then.

(MARK and LOTTIE write.)

TALK BACK!

1. If you had ESP, what would you do? Is it a good or bad thing?

2. What do you think your parents and siblings are thinking about you? Would you want to know?

3. If you could have one superpower, what would it be?

4. Do you think people communicate too much or too little about what they're thinking and feeling?

5. What do you think about Lottie using her new ability to cheat? Would you do it if you had the chance?

EARLY MAN

5F, 1M

WHO

FEMALES
> Eve
> Jasmine
> Kaylee
> Kitty
> Petra

MALES
> Thal

WHERE Scene 1: Outdoors; Scene 2: Eve's garage.

WHEN Present day.

🎭 Eve, Petra, Kitty: Try using a "substitution" for Thal. Instead of the actor before you, imagine he's someone in your life who you really, truly think is helpful and great.

✍ Write a play about how Kitty, Eve, and Petra found Thal in the first place.

Scene 1: The Plan

PETRA: Thal, I just don't know what to do. People think I'm smart. They expect a lot of me. But the pressure is really hard to deal with. I'm just a kid, right? I don't feel like doing everything well. Sometimes I just want to be sloppy and relaxed. But I don't even know how! You know what I mean, right?

(THAL smiles and grunts.)

PETRA: So what should I do? I'm sick of being perfect. I want someone else to take control. For once, I want to just sit back and relax. Can you understand that? Why am I even asking? Of course you do. It's so good to talk to someone who understands you. It makes you feel less alone. The thing I like most about you, Thal, is that you listen. I already feel better. I just know you're going to help me because you understand how I feel.

(THAL claps his hands together slowly and carefully like it's the first time he's ever done it as EVE and KITTY enter.)

PETRA: How come other boys can't be like you?

EVE: I think it's because Thal's parents must have brought him up differently, him being ancient man and all that. People must have been quieter and more polite back then.

PETRA: Can you imagine a whole world filled with real gentlemen like Thal here? Just changing Jesse Quavers and Rick Nippy would be a massive improvement on the world.

KITTY: I don't know if I've said this before, Thal, but thank you for never giving me a wet willy.

(THAL looks confused.)

KITTY: I mean it. I really appreciate it.

(THAL grunts.)

EVE: I just got the best idea! I can't even believe how smart I am. Yes, I can! I can believe it now since you've encouraged me so much, Thal. I have so much more confidence in myself. My self-esteem is through the roof.

PETRA: Your idea?

EVE: Right! Here it is. Brace yourselves. I think Thal here should teach lessons to other kids on how to behave. We really shouldn't keep him to ourselves, even though he is perfect.

KITTY: I like having Thal to ourselves. It's like having a walking jar opener!

PETRA: Not to mention our long talks. Is sharing Thal such a good idea?

EVE: Well, I hear what you're saying, you two. I hear what you're saying because Thal taught me to pay attention more, right Thal? You think that we wouldn't have as much time with Thal if we shared him. I understand. I do. I just wonder if we would be doing something great for the universe if we did this. This could be an automatic intro in heaven or something. I know you're Jewish and don't believe in heaven, Kitty, because you told me that last week and I was listening to you, but you must have some kind of similar thing. I'm just thinking this could be big. He could teach manners, listening skills, deportment, grooming—all kinds of things! And we could maybe charge a small fee for these services. So we could buy some cute stuff for ourselves and for Thal, too, of course! What could be better? We'd be making the world a better place *and* we'd be able to afford that trip to Africa to go on safari, too. Girls, we must do this. The world needs this. We need this. Thal needs this. We can't be selfish anymore! I have discovered a Purpose in Life!

PETRA: Isn't deportment what happens when they kick you out of the U.S.?

EVE: That's deportation. Deportment is how you walk and stuff.

KITTY: Are you sure?

EVE: Yes!

KITTY: I think Petra's right.

EVE: Whatever. You know what I'm saying.

PETRA: You don't believe in heaven, Kitty?

KITTY: We sort of have a heaven, but a different name. But it's more important to be good now, in the present moment. Or at least that's what my mom thinks. But that brings up a point. Eve, can we really be doing good in the world if we're getting paid for it?

EVE: We're still helping the world.

PETRA: But we're also helping us.

EVE: But we're also helping the world.

KITTY: But we're also doing it for selfish reasons.

EVE: But we're also helping the world! You can do both!

PETRA: Can you?

KITTY: What do you think, Thal?

(THAL scratches his head.)

PETRA: It's a tough question.

KITTY: You're so smart, Thal.

EVE: Don't you see? Thal could show people how to treat people and how to think, and we could do their hair and nails and all that. It could be like a beauty shop. But also with manners. Here. Let me show you an example. I come to see Thal. Hello, Thal.

(THAL waves.)

EVE: Thal, I never listen to anyone and I'm mean.

(THAL blows a raspberry.)

EVE: See? Kids can relate to Thal; he gets right to the point. Here's another example. Say I come in walking like this (EVE walks stiffly like a robot.) like Petra.

PETRA: Hey!

EVE: Thal, can you help me?

(THAL shuffles over to EVE, slouching.)

EVE: See? Thal knows how to walk right. He looks relaxed and cool.

PETRA: Is that what you think I should do, Thal?

(THAL waves at PETRA.)

PETRA: That is so smart! People will expect less of me if I look less upright. I won't seem so smart and capable. Thanks, Thal!

KITTY: Thal knows everything. You're the coolest, Thal.

EVE: Definitely. I used to walk upright before, and boy did my back hurt. Now that I'm slouching, I feel much better. All because of Thal! He's a genius!

(THAL starts running in circles like he's chasing his tail.)

KITTY: Aw! Look how excited he is!

PETRA: OK, Eve, let's do it!

EVE: Excellent!

(THAL falls over, dizzy. He stays lying on the ground.)

PETRA: We'll need some supplies.

KITTY: And we need advertising!

EVE: We should make signs.

PETRA: Thal can help us figure out what to say on them.

EVE: Of course, we need beauty supplies and a space to work in.

KITTY: My mom has a lot of makeup. She won't notice if some is missing. She might even donate some if I ask nicely. She sometimes lets me wear her stuff.

EVE: My brother plays with his band in our garage. If I have a fit, I bet my parents will let me use it, too. It's only fair. Why should he get to use the garage for his stuff and not me?

PETRA: So we've got supplies and a place and we'll make signs. I think we're in business!

KITTY: Thal, are you ready for this?

(THAL is still resting on the ground.)

KITTY: Sorry. He's resting.

EVE: Good! He's thinking ahead. He'll need some rest, once the business is up and running!

PETRA: Do you really think we could go on safari in Africa?

EVE: Can and will! You've seen how excited Thal gets when we watch the Discovery Channel. It's the least we can do.

KITTY: We need some paper and markers. Let's start making signs!

EVE: This is going to be a huge success! With Thal's help, we are going to change the world!

Scene 2: The (Cave) Man

(JASMINE enters. She is very well groomed and neat.)

JASMINE: I saw a really strange sign outside. It was just scribbles. What's going on in here?

EVE: Thal's abstract design got us our first customer!

KITTY: Thal always knows best.

PETRA: So, Jasmine, come in!

JASMINE: What's going on in here?

EVE: Welcome to Thal's Finishing School. We'll finish everything about you that's undone.

JASMINE: What do you mean? I think I'm done.

KITTY: It's like a beauty parlor but with manners, too.

JASMINE: Oh! That's cute. OK. So what do I do?

PETRA: Come sit in our chair while Thal thinks about what you need. Thal?

(THAL enters.)

JASMINE: Oh my God! What is that?

KITTY: Not *what*. Who!

JASMINE: Who is that?

EVE: That is Thal. The best, most amazing, smartest, most talented guy in the universe! He's also ancient man.

JASMINE: What?

PETRA: A Neanderthal.

JASMINE: I thought those evolved.

KITTY: Did they? Or did we devolve?

JASMINE: Is that even a word?

KITTY: Well, it is now.

JASMINE: What do you mean "devolve"?

PETRA: We've noticed that Thal listens more and is more polite than other boys—

KITTY: He never interrupts!

EVE: He's also very direct. You never have to guess what he's thinking.

PETRA: It's so much simpler.

KITTY: So maybe we've gone backward—devolved—instead of going forward.

EVE: Jasmine, we discovered Thal frozen in a nearby cave. We thawed him out—

JASMINE: Oh! That's how he got his name!

KITTY: No, not Thaw, Thal! Like Neanderthal!

JASMINE: Oh!

EVE: Anyway, as I was saying, we found Thal and thawed him out and discovered that he knew a lot more about stuff than we did. He's really got great self-esteem.

KITTY: He's got such a distinctive walk!

PETRA: He doesn't fuss too much with hair gel.

EVE: He knows just what to say and when to say it.

PETRA: He's just amazing! He knows everything!

KITTY: We all feel so much more confident.

EVE: So we had to share him with the world.

PETRA: And today, Jasmine, you are the first person to take advantage of Thal's amazingness.

JASMINE: I feel so lucky!

EVE: You should. You are about to be remade. Thal, what do you think?

(THAL circles JASMINE.)

JASMINE: I'm nervous.

PETRA: Don't be. Really. He knows what he's doing.

JASMINE: OK.

(THAL comes up behind JASMINE and suddenly

starts messing up her hair. JASMINE screams. THAL walks away from JASMINE and sits on the floor.)

PETRA: That's it!

KITTY: It's perfect!

JASMINE: What? What? What did he do to me?

EVE: Only improve you a million times over.

JASMINE: How? I don't even know what he did.

KITTY: He just knew exactly what to do.

JASMINE: What? What?

EVE: Let's do the finishing touches.

(KITTY, EVE, and PETRA take out brushes and start messing up JASMINE's hair more.)

JASMINE: I don't get this. What are you doing?

PETRA: Finishing you! Just stay still. You're nearly done.

KITTY: Ta-da!

EVE: You're done!

JASMINE: Let me see!

(KITTY pulls out a mirror and shows JASMINE her reflection. Her hair is very messed up.)

JASMINE: My hair! This is an improvement? You've got to be crazy. I look terrible! I can't believe you messed up my hair! I liked it how it was! Now I don't know if it will ever be the same. How could you do this? I never thought my hair was that important to me, but now . . . Now I *know* it's important! I mean, it's right on top of my head; it's practically the first thing you see. I just don't know what to do! How could you? What will I tell my mother? I hope she won't notice. She always tells me how good my hair looks when it's nice and neat. I am going to be in so much trouble! I'm sorry to be mad about this and I don't want to be a baby, but I just can't believe it!

PETRA: I like you so much better now.

EVE: You look relaxed.

KITTY: And so glamorous!

PETRA: Thal always knows what to do. He fixed my walk!

(KAYLEE enters. She is very cool and relaxed—in fact, she appears to be half asleep.)

JASMINE: I don't know about—

KAYLEE: Jasmine! I love your hair!

JASMINE: You love it? I look better? Seriously? Maybe I just don't know what's nice. Are you sure? Is . . . is it glamorous?

KAYLEE: It's sassy and fun!

JASMINE: **Thanks!**

KITTY: See?

JASMINE: **Thal, you're a genius!**

EVE: Don't just thank him; pay him!

(JASMINE takes out some money.)

JASMINE: Well, I've only got my allowance money—

(EVE takes the money from JASMINE's hand.)

EVE: That will do!

JASMINE: Thanks! Bye!

KAYLEE: What's going on? Is this a beauty shop?

PETRA: Sort of. It's that and more.

KAYLEE: Excellent! So, fix me up! I love a good makeover.

(KITTY, PETRA, and EVE step away from KAYLEE.)

KITTY: This is going to be hard.

PETRA: She's quite a challenge.

EVE: She's already cool, isn't she?

PETRA: I wonder what Thal will do.

KITTY: Well, he'll know what's best.

EVE: I can't wait to see what he does!

KAYLEE: Should I sit?

PETRA: Sure!

KITTY: Thal? Thal!

(THAL's napping and snoring loudly.)

EVE: Thal!

(THAL awakens with a start.)

PETRA: Thal, Kaylee here needs your help.

(THAL stands and roars, angry at being awakened. KAYLEE is wide-eyed and frightened.)

KAYLEE: Aaaaaah! What is that?

EVE: Kaylee, I never knew you had such pretty eyes!

KITTY: You are so right!

KAYLEE: I do?

PETRA: When you open them up wide like that, you can really see the color.

KAYLEE: Really?

EVE: Completely!

(KAYLEE looks in the mirror.)

KAYLEE: You're right!

KITTY: I knew Thal would know what you needed.

KAYLEE: Wow! So that was all an act.

PETRA: Definitely. Thal always knows what's best.

KAYLEE: Wow. I am going to tell all my friends about him!

PETRA: Please do!

EVE: That will be five dollars.

KAYLEE: OK! It was worth every penny. Thanks, Thal! Know what? I actually think I learned something, can you believe it? I thought your friend here was some kind of creep because he's not evolved. But the fact is he's really excellent. He improved both my looks and my outlook! Now that my eyes have been opened, I see the world more clearly. It's a sunny day and there's so much I can do! For one thing, I want to tell all my friends about your cave-man friend. I guess since he's not all caught up in all the silly things in the world like stickers and books and shoes and school, he can concentrate on what's important. Like seeing people with clear eyes and trying to help people out. Just one thing—do you think he could wear a shirt? I mean, now that he's helped me, I just want to pass on some advice, too. I'm not sure it's sanitary for him to walk around shirtless like that. Plus, it's cold outside. It's a little bit wacko, even for someone who's pre-historic. Just a thought.

(THAL growls at KAYLEE.)

KAYLEE: Aaaaah! Oh, thanks for the reminder, Thal.

PETRA: We'll take your ideas into advisement. But it might not be what's right for Thal.

KAYLEE: Of course. It was just an idea. Well, see ya!

EVE: Tell your friends!

KITTY: Another job well done. I feel so good about myself today. We are truly decent and giving people thanks to you Thal.

(THAL belches.)

EVE: You always know just what to say.

TALK BACK!

1. Do you ever talk to your pets or someone/something that can't talk back? Why?

2. Do you think you're judgmental about people's intelligence based on their looks?

3. Do you tend to see the positive or the negative side of things? For example, the girls in the play saw the positive side to Thal's scaring Kaylee. Would you?

4. What did you think of Thal's makeovers? Are they really improvements?

5. Is it possible to do a really unselfish act? Or is it selfish if you get satisfaction or payment for what you do (even if it does help people)?

6. What was life like in Thal's time? Would you want to live back then? Why or why not?

OLD

3F, 2M

WHO

FEMALES	MALES
Jada	Dad
Mom	Jason
Steph	

WHERE At home. Scene 1: Evening; Scene 2: Morning.

WHEN Present day.

🎭 Listen carefully to how the other actors say their lines and respond to them based on your observations. For example, if another actor says something in a way that annoys you, respond like you're annoyed with him or her!

✍ Take one feature about you and change it. For example, think about what it would be like to be very, very tall or to have a really long tongue. Then write about it.

Scene 1: Mature

(JASON enters.)

MOM: Where have you been? I thought you were coming right home after school.

JASON: I was with the guys.

MOM: Who are these guys?

JASON: You know, the guys. Same old guys.

MOM: Old guys?

JASON: The guys I've known forever. Will you stop with the questions, Mom?

MOM: Jason, I want to know where you were and whom you were with and why you were not home when you said you would be. These are reasonable questions. Your safety is important to me.

JASON: Fine. I was in Mike's backyard with Mike and Bill and Darren. We were playing baseball. We lost track of time. So I'm late. OK?

MOM: Not OK. I worry about you when you disappear. Do you understand that? You should be a little more considerate. Grow up a little, Jason.

JASON: I'm plenty grown up. Jeez, Mom.

MOM: I'm serious, young man.

JASON: Fine, Mom!

MOM: Next time maybe you can come home first and say, "Mom, may I please go play baseball in Mike's backyard with Mike, Bill, and Derek?"

JASON: Darren, Mom. The other guy is Darren.

MOM: Fine, Darren. Did you hear me, though? Are you listening?

JASON: Yeah, yeah.

MOM: Don't "yeah, yeah" me, young man! This is serious. Next time you ask permission and tell me where you're going to be and who you'll be with, do you understand?

JASON: Yeah, sure.

MOM: Jason, this is no joke. I mean it. Your dad will be home soon. Maybe he can get this through your head. I've got enough on my hands taking care of little Jada.

JASON: Yeah, so I thought you wouldn't care if I played baseball with my friends. You're busy with Jada anyway.

MOM: You know that I still want to know where you are, Jason—

JASON: OK, OK! Can we leave it alone now?

(DAD enters.)

MOM: Oh, good, you're home.

DAD: Looks like it!

MOM: Maybe you can explain to your son why he can't just do anything he wants without consulting us.

DAD: Will do.

(MOM *exits.*)

DAD: What's going on, son?

JASON: Nothing.

DAD: Nothing? Your mom seems to think it's something.

JASON: It's so boring. I just went and played baseball after school with my friends, that's all.

DAD: OK. That's it?

JASON: Yep.

DAD: Well, that does seem OK.

JASON: See?

DAD: So why is your mother concerned?

JASON: Dunno.

DAD: Honey, why are you cross with Jason?

(MOM *enters with little sister JADA.*)

MOM: Did he tell you what he did? Jada, stop squirming. Hold Mommy's hand.

DAD: He said he went to play baseball.

JADA: Daddy!

DAD: Jada!

(*JADA goes to DAD. She's hyper.*)

JADA: Daddy! Daddy! Dad, Dad, Dad!

DAD: Hello, Jada!

MOM: He didn't say anything else?

JADA: Daddy!

DAD: No. What else is there?

MOM: Jada, come to Mommy, honey.

JADA: No!

MOM: Jada, come to Mommy! We're going to take a bath now.

JADA: No!

MOM: Jada, come here now!

(*JADA comes to MOM reluctantly.*)

JADA: I don't wanna.

MOM: That's a good girl. It will be fun!

JADA: No!

DAD: Honey? About Jason?

MOM: Jason disappeared this afternoon and didn't tell me where he was going or who he was playing with. He doesn't seem to understand that I worry about him and that it's important for him to be more mature about these things.

JADA: Daddy!

DAD: That's a good girl, Jada. Go with Mommy.

JADA: No! Daddy!

DAD: No, honey. Daddy will see you later. Daddy needs to talk to Jason.

JASON: That's OK, Dad. I get it. Go ahead.

DAD: No, we're going to have a talk.

JADA: Jason!

JASON: Hello, Jada.

JADA: Up!

MOM: No, Jada. We're going to take a bath now.

JADA: NO!

MOM: Yes, honey. You can play later.

JADA: No!

(*MOM drags JADA out of the room.*)

DAD: Now your little sister can get away with acting like that because she's a baby. You're much older, though.

JASON: Duh.

DAD: Jason, don't give me any attitude.

JASON: But I wasn't doing anything wrong! I was playing a sport with my friends. What's so bad about that? Why is this such a federal case?

DAD: Your mom worries about you. I worry about you. We're just concerned about your safety. A lot of things could happen to you just wandering around. You could be kidnapped or in an accident . . . so we need to know where you are. Also something might happen where we need to find you. Like, say, the house catches fire and we don't know where you are. Where's Jason? Is he in his room? Is he in the house?

JASON: I get it, OK? Enough!

DAD: Your mom seems to think this isn't getting through to you. And I think she's right. This isn't a joke or a game. This is serious, Jason.

JASON: Fine! I get it! I was just playing baseball with my friends. I don't see the big deal. But, FINE, I'll tell you from now on every time I'm going to go somewhere or do something. OK?

DAD: OK. But I'd like a little less attitude, young man.

JASON: Argh! Fine!

(STEPH knocks on the door.)

STEPH: Jason!

(*JASON opens the door and STEPH enters.*)

STEPH: Hey, J, wanna come over to my house and play video games?

JASON: Hold on. Dad, can I go over to Steph's and play video games? Do you need to know the video games we'll be playing?

DAD: What did I say about attitude?

JASON: So, can I?

DAD: Yes, you may.

(*DAD exits.*)

STEPH: What was that?

JASON: My parents are on this big kick where I have to tell them everything: where I'm going, who I'm going with, when I'll be back . . . Practically everything. Pretty soon I'll have to ask them if I can go to the bathroom. It's so stupid because what do we do anyway? The same old stuff. It's always the same stuff. Play baseball or video games or watch TV or eat or just sit around. So what's the big deal? Why is everything always so dramatic? "We worry about you, Jason!" It's embarrassing. Why do parents have to be like that? Why can't they just take it easy?

STEPH: Dunno.

JASON: They tell me I have to be more mature and grown up. I'm a kid still. Why would I want to do that? Plus, the exact opposite is true. Adults never have to tell other adults what they're doing and all that. If an adult wants to go get pretzels at the store, they just go. They don't turn to anyone who's standing around to say, "Please, may I go to the store? Would it be OK?" A man doesn't call his mom in Arizona to tell her that he's thinking pretzels, is that OK?

STEPH: It would be funny if he did. Can you imagine if adults had to ask us for everything? That would be excellent. "Steph, I was thinking of making chicken for dinner tonight. Is that OK?" "No, Mom, make macaroni and cheese." "OK, Steph. It will be ready at six." "No, I want it now, Mom." Things would be great if we were in charge. We would go on vacation all the time, and I'd never have to explain why I punched my brother.

JASON: Sounds good.

STEPH: I'd make my mom do my chores or at least lay off asking me to do them. And can you imagine them asking our permission for things? "Steph, I'm going to work on my computer now." "What sites will you be looking at, Dad? I need to know the content and the addresses." I can see them getting all whiny and pathetic. Man, we must be annoying!

JASON: But we wouldn't be if *they* weren't so annoying.

STEPH: True. We wouldn't be annoying if we didn't have to be. If they didn't make us. It's too bad parents don't see that.

JASON: Yeah. Too bad. They'll never get it.

Scene 2: Immature

(Next day. JASON enters the kitchen.)

JASON: Hey, where is everybody? Is it Saturday? Hello? What's going on? Can anyone hear me? *(Beat.)* This is creepy. Mom? Where are you?

(JADA enters.)

JASON: Mom, Jada is in the kitchen. Hello? What's going on here? Seriously, this isn't funny. And I'm hungry. Jada, go find Mommy.

JADA: No!

JASON: Jada, don't be bad. Now go find Mommy. Then we can have breakfast.

JADA: No!

JASON: Jada, you're a brat.

(JADA screams.)

JASON: Jada, shut up!

JADA: Nooooo!

JASON: Jada! Mom! Jada won't shut up! *(Beat.)* Jada, aren't you hungry? Wouldn't you like some food?

JADA: Yes!

JASON: Well, Mommy can make you breakfast. Go find Mommy!

JADA: Mommy's sleeping. You make breakfast.

JASON: I don't know how to make breakfast.

JADA: Jason! I'm hungry!

JASON: So am I!

JADA: Food!

JASON: Mommy makes food. Go find Mommy!

(*JADA sits down and cries.*)

JASON: Mom! Help!

(*MOM stumbles in wearing pajamas and takes a seat at the breakfast table.*)

MOM: What's all the noise about? I'm trying to sleep.

JASON: You're supposed to make us breakfast before school. We're running late.

MOM: So?

JASON: So? Do something!

MOM: I don't feel like it.

JASON: It doesn't matter if you feel like it. It's your job.

MOM: Nah.

JASON: Are you sick or something?

JADA: Mommy!

MOM: Jason, will you get Jada to be quiet?

JASON: What?

MOM: Jada wants something.

JASON: You're the mom here.

MOM: I'm tired.

JASON: What's going on here?

(DAD enters.)

DAD: Jason, I want waffles.

JASON: Me, too.

DAD: Excellent. Waffles it is.

(DAD sits. Beat.)

JASON: You don't expect me to make them?

DAD: Who else?

JASON: How about you or Mom?

DAD: Nah.

JASON: Is this some kind of test? Because I get it, OK? You made your point.

DAD: Point?

MOM: I'm hungry.

JADA: So hungry!

DAD: So, so hungry.

(MOM, DAD, and JADA all sit looking at JASON.)

JASON: You're kidding, right? *(Beat.)* Well, you can forget about it. Get your own breakfast.

(DAD gets up and takes out a box of cookies.)

JASON: You can't eat that.

DAD: Why not?

JASON: It's not good for you. Plus, they're mine.

DAD: Your name's not on them.

JASON: They're my favorite. Mom bought them for me.

MOM: No, I didn't.

JASON: Yes, you did.

MOM: Well, I want them.

JASON: You can't have them.

MOM: I can do whatever I want.

JASON: No, you can't.

DAD: I'm getting out of here. This place stinks.

JASON: Well, I'm going with you.

DAD: No, you're not.

JASON: So I'm not going to school?

DAD: What do I care?

JASON: Well, you're supposed to care. You usually care.

DAD: Well then, I guess today's the exception. I'm outta here.

JASON: Seriously, are you going to work?

DAD: I don't know. Stop asking me questions! You're always telling me what to do!

JASON: I never tell you what to do. Or at least you never listen.

DAD: Give me a break. You do, too. I hate this place!

(DAD exits, slamming the door behind him.)

JASON: What was that?

JADA: You made Daddy mad.

JASON: Dad is crazy. I don't know what's going on here. If this is a joke, it isn't funny anymore. This is nuts. Things are not supposed to go this way. You're supposed to be in charge. I'm just a kid. I don't want to be in charge. Things are going to go really bad when it's time to pay the bills, I hope you know. And if nobody in this family works, we won't have any money anyway. So whatever this is, it's got to stop. Mom, you and Dad are going to have to start acting like adults again. You made your point. I see why you're bossy all the time and tell me what to do. I get it. You can stop now. I'm not going to make you breakfast or take care of Jada. That's your job, just like telling me what to do and bossing me around is your job. OK? *I get it.* So quit already! Are you even listening to me?

MOM: I'm hungry.

JASON: The world's turned upside-down!

(*STEPH knocks on the door.*)

JASON: Mom, aren't you going to answer that?

MOM: I'm not supposed to answer the door.

JASON: Fine! I'll do it. And if it's a kidnapper, I hope you'll be happy.

(*JASON opens the door as MOM and JADA eat cookies.*)

JASON: I told you those are my cookies!

MOM: Your name's not on them.

JADA: Mmm, cookies.

(*STEPH enters.*)

STEPH: Sorry I'm late. I had to get everyone dressed and fed and Matthew had to be driven to daycare.

JASON: You drove a car?

STEPH: You say that like I don't do it every day.

JASON: You don't. You've never driven a car in your life.

STEPH: Jason, you slay me.

JASON: Do you want to play video games? Looks like I'm not going to school.

STEPH: You sound like your dad when he comes by to play with Matthew.

JASON: What? My dad plays with Matthew, your little brother?

STEPH: No, your dad plays with Matthew, my dad. They play video games every afternoon. So, want a ride to work?

JASON: Work?

STEPH: You know, the place where we sit behind a desk and do business.

JASON: I don't even know which is worse—you working or you driving a car!

STEPH: I'm an excellent driver.

JASON: Right, right.

STEPH: You realize your mother and Jada are eating cookies for breakfast.

JASON: Yeah. I told them to make themselves something, but they didn't listen. (*To MOM.*) Stop being a pig! Leave some for me!

MOM: You called me a pig! You're so mean!

(*MOM runs out of the room.*)

JADA: Meanie!

JASON: Shut up, Jada.

(*JADA cries.*)

JASON: Oh, jeez.

STEPH: Well, it looks like you've got your hands full here. I guess I'll be going.

JASON: Fine, fine, whatever. I hope my parents paid you a lot to go through with this game.

STEPH: You really are acting quite odd today, Jason. Will I see you at work then?

JASON: Oh, yeah. You bet.

(*STEPH exits. JASON watches her go.*)

JASON: She's really driving!

JADA: Jaaaaason!

JASON: **Please tell me I'm dreaming! I don't want to be an adult! I want to be a kid. But I'll be more grown up, I promise! Just make my life go back to** the way it was. Make Mom act like a mom and nag me about where I am and make breakfast and yell at me for being late. I might still complain sometimes about it, but I'll try not to. And Dad can call me "young man" in that really annoying way and expect me to be better at sports and tell me to clean the garage. I probably still won't want to, but I will. I swear. I will. If you please, please, please make things go back to normal. Listen, this whole family will go right down the toilet if I'm in charge here. Jada will starve and her teeth will fall out—

(JADA *cries again.*)

JASON: —and we won't have any money and the house will be a mess . . . This just really isn't a good idea! So whoever's in charge, make things go back to how they used to be!

(DAD *enters, dressed in work clothes.*)

DAD: Son, why aren't you ready for school?

JASON: I was trying to find breakfast for Jada and you left—

DAD: Where's your mom?

JASON: Upstairs. She's mad at me.

DAD: Honey?

(MOM *enters, dressed for the day.*)

MOM: I finally found that black sock you lost.

DAD: Great! Jason says he's trying to make breakfast for Jada.

MOM: Jason, you know she's not supposed to eat cookies in the morning!

JADA: Mommy!

MOM: Mommy's going to make you some nice oatmeal, Jada.

JADA: Yay!

JASON: Sorry, Mom. Really. I'm really sorry.

MOM: OK, OK. Just run upstairs and get ready for school.

JASON: Great! Fantastic! I'll hurry! (*Beat.*) Dad? Do you play video games every afternoon with Steph's dad?

DAD: I hate video games. You know that.

JASON: That is so great, Dad. So great!

(*JASON exits.*)

MOM: You know, sometimes I just don't understand that boy.

TALK BACK!

1. Do you think you should be treated more like an adult? If so, how?

2. What do you hate being nagged about? Do you think it's right? Do you think it's necessary? What would work better?

3. Do you want to be older? Why or why not?

4. What are the advantages of being a kid rather than growing up quickly?

5. How would you change things if you were in charge?

6. Which is worse: being in charge of everything or nothing? Are adult responsibilities a burden?

7. What is stressful about going into your teen years?

INVISIBLE EYE FOR THE NERD GUY

6F, 6M

WHO:

FEMALES	MALES
Autumn	Charlie
Celine	Fred
Kim	Leroy
Michelle	Mark
Tami	Robbie
Teacher	Todd

WHERE Various locations around school.

WHEN Scene 1: Monday; Scene 2: Tuesday.

🎭 Know your objective. Your objective is what you want most in a scene. Never forget your objective! It's what makes acting look real compared to just reading off lines.

🖋 Write your own guide telling people how to be invisible.

Scene 1: The Disappearance

(CHARLIE sits in the center of a classroom.)

CHARLIE: *(Standing.)* This is about the day I became invisible.

(CHARLIE sits. TEACHER stands in front of the kids.)

TEACHER: Who knows the answer to my question?

(CHARLIE, and only CHARLIE, raises his hand and grows increasingly frantic.)

TEACHER: *(Looking around.)* Anyone? Anyone at all? No one in this room can answer my question?

(TEACHER sits. CHARLIE stands again.)

CHARLIE: See? It just gets worse. One day, with no warning at all, everything started to go wrong. Or right. Well, different.

(MICHELLE and MARK stand. When a name is called out, someone from the group stands and exits.)

MICHELLE: Robbie.

MARK: Todd.

MICHELLE: Kim.

MARK: Leroy.

MICHELLE: Autumn.

MARK: Celine.

MICHELLE: Tami.

MARK: *(Reluctantly.)* Fred, I guess.

(Everyone's been picked except CHARLIE.)

MARK: I guess that's it. Let's play!

(MARK and MICHELLE exit. CHARLIE sits alone.)

CHARLIE: What's going on? I really couldn't figure it out. Suddenly, no one seemed to notice me anymore. Like I just wasn't there. I started to wonder if I actually existed.

(KIM, AUTUMN, MICHELLE, and CELINE enter. CHARLIE goes over to stand right beside KIM.)

KIM: Boys are so stupid.

AUTUMN: I know!

CELINE: I wish we didn't have to have anything to do with them.

KIM: I don't even want to be near one!

AUTUMN: But still, you know you like Robbie.

KIM: I wish I didn't.

MICHELLE: But you do.

KIM: Remember, I swore you guys to secrecy. No one is

ever supposed to know. Especially since I sent him that note. No one is ever allowed to know!

CELINE: You don't want him to ever know?

KIM: Never!

AUTUMN: Not even if he likes you back? I think he might like you back.

KIM: He pushed me in softball!

MICHELLE: Maybe he pushed you because he likes you.

KIM: I never understood that. I don't think that's actually true.

CELINE: Maybe he did it to get your attention.

KIM: That doesn't make any sense to me. Why would anyone be horrible to you if they want your attention? If they *like* you? I think parents tell us that to make us feel better. If a girl pushed me, no one would say, "Maybe she wants to be your friend." Why do people think that when it's a boy? If I liked someone I'd try being nice to him. Give him some compliments, maybe. That's what I'd like. Just like in the movies. I certainly wouldn't act like a bully. No, Robbie hates me. He was just trying to be mean. *Especially* because I was trying to be nice to him. He was going out of his way to be a jerk. No other explanation makes sense.

CELINE: Boys don't make sense, though.

MICHELLE: Didn't you ever want to do something, anything to someone to get them to pay attention to you?

KIM: I guess sometimes I might want to do something like punch Robbie to get his attention. But I don't because that's crazy. Boys are crazy. And why would we have that instinct anyway? It's so caveman; it's embarrassing. Haven't we evolved at all as a species?

AUTUMN: So how come you didn't sign the note?

KIM: In case something like this happened. Plus, I wrote totally personal things in the note. Plus, I'd know he liked me back if he could tell or wanted it to be me who wrote it.

CELINE: But what if he can recognize your handwriting?

KIM: He won't.

MICHELLE: But if he does?

KIM: He can't! I wrote totally personal things in that note. He just can't!

AUTUMN: You put it in his locker? Maybe he hasn't seen it yet.

CELINE: Yeah! Maybe we could get it.

KIM: How? His locker is *locked*.

MICHELLE: I'm so glad I don't like anyone in our class. It makes life so complicated.

AUTUMN: I wouldn't want any of the boys in our class within ten feet of me if I had the choice.

KIM: Love stinks.

(CHARLIE *tentatively reaches out and pokes AUTUMN. She doesn't react. CHARLIE then puts his whole hand on her head while she says the following line. She does not acknowledge him at all.*)

AUTUMN: Well, let's see what we can do about that note.

(ROBBIE, TODD, *and* LEROY *enter. ROBBIE pretends to open a locker.*)

KIM: I don't know what to do! How can we get close?

CELINE: I have no idea! This is going to be harder than I thought.

(ROBBIE, TODD, MARK, *and* LEROY *stand in a tight group blocking the "locker." CHARLIE walks right up, reaches his hand in the middle of the group and comes out with a folded note in his hand.*)

KIM: Oh God! I'd love to be invisible! This is impossible!

MICHELLE: Maybe we should distract them.

(*While the girls plot,* CHARLIE *reads the letter and is amused and amazed by what he reads.*)

CELINE: How?

(AUTUMN *falls to the ground.*)

AUTUMN: Ow! My ankle!

(The boys don't respond.)

AUTUMN: OW! MY ANKLE!

CELINE: *(Loudly.)* Oh, look! Autumn hurt her ankle! Who can help? We need help!

TODD: One of you should get the nurse.

AUTUMN: They're so stupid.

MICHELLE: Todd, maybe you could help.

TODD: You have legs.

AUTUMN: I need to get to class. Some strong people have to take me.

(ROBBIE, TODD, MARK, and LEROY all stare at her.)

ROBBIE: Fine. I'll just close my locker—

KIM/CELINE/AUTUMN: No!

(ROBBIE shuts his locker.)

ROBBIE: OK. Todd, pick up Autumn.

TODD: I can't pick her up!

MARK: You should go to the nurse, not to class.

(AUTUMN jumps up.)

AUTUMN: Actually, I think it was a minor sprain. I feel better.

LEROY: Weird. It's like a miracle or something.

ROBBIE: Let's go, then.

TODD: Girls are crazy, man.

(LEROY, TODD, MARK, and ROBBIE exit.)

KIM: It's hopeless! I'll never get that note!

(KIM, CELINE, MICHELLE, and AUTUMN exit.)

CHARLIE: This note is excellent! There's enough dirt in here to blackmail Kim forever. But how come no one is noticing me? Am I really invisible? And if I am, what can I do about it? Do I want to do anything about it? Or do I want to enjoy it? Think of all the things I can do: listen in on private conversations, steal things, never go to school—Is this a good thing or not? And what do I do with this note? I can't help thinking there's a reason I have it. There's got to be one perfect thing that I can do with this information. But what? Kim isn't the nicest person, once she told a girl I liked her just to mean—I didn't like her *at all*, she was just trying to humiliate me—but I don't think I want to blackmail her, either. This note actually makes me like her more. 'Cause her life isn't great either, I guess. For some reason, I thought everybody's life was great except mine. Well, I think I'll go home and take a nap. I'll figure all this out tomorrow.

Scene 2: Supernerd Lives!

CHARLIE: Today's the day I figure out what to do with my invisibility.

(ROBBIE, TODD, MARK, and LEROY return, dragging FRED behind them. They stop right next to Charlie.)

LEROY: Get moving!

FRED: I don't want to go in the lockers again! Don't you ever get sick of that?

CHARLIE: They used to do that to me all the time.

TODD: No.

ROBBIE: Never. We can beat you up first.

FRED: Oh, come on, guys. Give me a break. There are three of you; it's not fair.

CHARLIE: That's not going to stop them. Trust me.

TODD: Hey, why don't we hang his pants on the flagpole?

LEROY: Great idea! We've never done that!

MARK: Do you know how to use the flagpole?

LEROY: We can figure that out, right?

LEROY: It can't be that hard.

FRED: You're going to take my pants off? That's sick!

ROBBIE: That'll teach you not to cover your paper during a test.

FRED: I didn't want you to cheat off of me!

ROBBIE: Exactly, nerd.

TODD: Let's take him outside.

(TODD, LEROY, MARK, and ROBBIE start to drag FRED offstage.)

FRED: Come on. Give me a break. I won't do it again! *(To CHARLIE.)* Help me!

CHARLIE: Are you talking to me? *(To audience.)* Was he talking to me? I thought I was invisible. Why could that guy see me? None of the girls see me. They've been saying a lot of secrets right in front of me. Like today, Angela is mad at Miranda because she has the same sweater as Angela and she already knew that Angela had it even though she hasn't worn it to school yet so now everyone's going to think that Angela copied Miranda when it's really the other way around. Did you know girls talk like that? Seriously, they do. And the guys don't notice me—at least the popular guys. No one's beat me up or called me a name all day. Teachers don't see me. I danced on Mrs. Pullman's desk this morning during quiet reading time. So how come that guy saw me? Do nerds have special vision? If so, how come they don't see a wedgie coming in time?

(TAMI enters, clearly upset.)

TAMI: No one even knows I'm alive. No one cares, either! I hate this school. I hate everything!

(TAMI looks up and sees CHARLIE.)

TAMI: What are you looking at?

CHARLIE: So much for the girl theory.

TAMI: What? You're not making any sense.

CHARLIE: I thought I was invisible to girls.

TAMI: That's stupid. I can see you perfectly well.

CHARLIE: You're not very nice, are you?

TAMI: Sure I am. I'm always nice, and I'm sick of it. What did it ever get me, being nice? People just take advantage. All I've ever done is try to be friends with people. I try so hard, you wouldn't even understand. I'll do anything—make someone's bed, do any dare, tell them nice things *all* the time—but it doesn't make any difference. People are just jerks. I hate everyone. Including you.

CHARLIE: You don't even know me.

TAMI: I've never even seen you before. But that doesn't matter. I have a whole new outlook on the world ever since—well, since today.

CHARLIE: What happened today?

TAMI: I don't want to talk any more about it. It's just—

It's just—really, really, *really* embarrassing. You wouldn't understand.

CHARLIE: Are you kidding? I'm the king of humiliation.

TAMI: Promise you won't tell anyone?

CHARLIE: OK. I promise. Who would I tell? I'm invisible to most everyone.

TAMI: They—a bunch of girls in my grade—took a picture of me . . . in my . . . underwear and they're showing it around the school. It's beyond embarrassing. I just don't want to exist anymore.

CHARLIE: I can help you with that.

TAMI: You can?

CHARLIE: I think so.

TAMI: How?

CHARLIE: Well, like I said, I'm invisible to most everyone now. I think only nerds, geeks, and losers can see me.

TAMI: Thanks a lot!

CHARLIE: Well, sorry, but it would explain why you didn't see me before today.

TAMI: I guess. But I'm not a nerd or a geek or a loser.

CHARLIE: What are you then?

TAMI: Maybe . . . an outcast.

CHARLIE: OK. I'll add that to my list.

TAMI: So? Tell me your secret.

CHARLIE: Let me think it through. I just realized I was invisible yesterday, so this might take me a minute.

(A few beats go by as CHARLIE thinks.)

CHARLIE: Got it! I gave up! I gave in. And I got a new haircut.

(FRED stumbles in rubbing his backside. ROBBIE, LEROY, and TODD trail behind.)

LEROY: Well, at least we gave him an atomic wedgie.

ROBBIE: We'll have to learn how to use the flagpole.

TODD: Next time.

(FRED sits down near TAMI and CHARLIE; TODD, LEROY, and ROBBIE exit.)

FRED: That hurt. Thanks a lot, by the way. You were a big help.

CHARLIE: Like you would have helped me. What could I have done?

FRED: I dunno. I guess you're right.

TAMI: So he can see you, too? But no one else can.

CHARLIE: Doesn't seem like it.

FRED: What's going on?

TAMI: This kid—

CHARLIE: I'm Charlie—

TAMI: —was telling me he's invisible.

FRED: What?

TAMI: He became invisible and now he's going to tell me how.

FRED: Aren't you the girl in that picture—

TAMI: Oh my God! I want to die!

CHARLIE: OK! OK! Be quiet now because I think I have the answer. *(To Fred.)* You'll want to know this, too.

FRED: Go on, then.

CHARLIE: The day I became invisible, yesterday, I stopped caring and I got a haircut.

(Beat.)

TAMI: So? What else?

CHARLIE: I think that's it. I wasn't mad anymore at all the bullies; I was too tired to be mad. And I didn't care if anyone liked me. I decided to just like being alone. I would just daydream when people I didn't like came near me instead of getting tense.

I became, like, a blob instead of a kid. It was almost like I thought myself invisible. If anyone started to pay attention to me, I just went away. I wasn't scared and I wasn't angry and I wasn't good and I wasn't bad and I wasn't too weird and I wasn't cool at all. I was just in the middle, nothing, all the time. Invisible! Plus, before I had a haircut like a newscaster, you know, really flat and combed and all that—

TAMI: I remember you now! You got locked in a locker once.

CHARLIE: Right! So I went to a new barber and he did my hair differently. It's not great, but it's not so geeky. My mom hates it. I think it's key that your parents should think you're a little odd if the kids at school are going to think you're normal.

TAMI: So how's that supposed to help me?

CHARLIE: You're too visible now because you care what those girls think about you. Maybe if you were like, "Yeah. That's my underwear. I think it's cute," maybe they would lay off you.

FRED: It was cute underwear. *(Embarrassed.)* I mean, I guess! It had flowers on it!

TAMI: Shut up, geek!

CHARLIE: See, you still want everyone to like you. That makes you visible. You try too hard. The popular kids can tell that you'll let them get away with anything. Like you'll probably forgive them immediately for what they did.

TAMI: Well, if they apologized . . .

FRED: Are you serious?

TAMI: But if I don't forgive them, then where will I be?

CHARLIE: Then you'll have power over them. They'll want to get you back in their circle. You'll be in control.

TAMI: I guess that would be good. But I don't know if I'm strong enough to do that. What if they just decided not to bother with me?

FRED: Look at how they're treating you now. How could it get worse?

TAMI: I don't know . . . I'd really hate to be ignored.

CHARLIE: You have to work through it. And other people will talk to you.

FRED: Get some *real* friends.

TAMI: At least I *have* friends.

FRED: You don't have to be cruel.

CHARLIE: You can do it, Tami. Look—I'm proof!

(*A bunch of kids enter. CHARLIE starts going completely nuts—singing, dancing, yelping, and jumping up and down. None of the kids react; the kids exit.*)

CHARLIE: See? I'm totally invisible.

FRED: But that doesn't make sense. You were trying to get their attention.

CHARLIE: Nah. Not exactly. The important part is I didn't care if they make fun of me if they saw me. I've been made fun of so many times I don't think there's anything more they could say that I haven't heard before.

FRED: But what about me?

CHARLIE: This is easy. I've been you. You need a makeover. A new haircut, for starters. Then, maybe wear a T-shirt instead of a button-down shirt tucked in and buttoned all the way up.

FRED: How am I supposed to get my mother to buy me all new things?

CHARLIE: You must have T-shirts for the summer and weekends, right?

FRED: Right.

CHARLIE: So, you wear them under your other shirt and then unbutton or take off the button-down shirt when you get to school.

TAMI: Girls do that kind of stuff all the time.

FRED: Oh! I get it!

CHARLIE: And you have to stop snorting when you laugh. You can still be yourself; you just have to be less extreme. I'm a nerd; I'll always be a nerd. But as long as I'm not the biggest, most obvious nerd, I'm OK. As long as I don't get upset or angry or sad that other people make fun of me or don't like me, I'm not a good target anymore. The bullies want to see you suffer. If you don't suffer, they're not interested in you.

TAMI: You are really wise.

CHARLIE: (*To the audience.*) Suddenly, in that moment, I became . . . SUPERNERD! My power is, obviously, invisibility and the ability to assist nerds everywhere. I've even thought about wearing my underpants on the outside, like Superman. Maybe I will, who knows? I guess I'll be seeing you. Oh, don't look surprised. You see me now, don't you? I'm not invisible to you, and you know what that means. Are you a geek, a nerd, a loser, or an outcast? Doesn't matter to me. But if you're in trouble, if you find yourself surrounded by the tag football team in the locker room or called names like Skinny Ginny or Farty Barty, I'll be there. Thank you, and good day.

TALK BACK!

1. Do you think it's good to try to be invisible like Charlie?

2. What do you think of Charlie's advice to Tami and Fred? Is it good or bad? Why?

3. Why do some people act like bullies?

4. What's the best way to deal with a bully?

5. What makes someone a target for a bully?

6. Why is one smart person labeled "popular" and another labeled a "nerd"?

7. Does it feel good or bad to go unnoticed?

8. Is it possible to make your parents happy *and* fit in at school at the same time? What's the trick?

THE ICE PALACE

5F, 5M

WHO

FEMALES	MALES
Aneesa	Flick
Giddy	Orlando
Lucy	Pull
Ping	Shane
Queen	Tip

WHERE Scene 1: The surface of a planet; Scene 2: The ice palace.

WHEN The future.

🎭 Explorers: Make your acting as real and natural as possible. Aliens: Feel free to be as unusual as you wish, as long as you're true to your character and your character's purpose in the play or scene. If the Explorers are realistic, then the otherworldly people will be more believable, too.

✍ Write a piece of science fiction. What is your new world like? How is it the same from Earth? How is it different? All plays need conflict. An easy way to include conflict is to put "normal" people in a strange, new situation.

Scene 1: Landing

LUCY: Quiet, everyone. We don't know what we're going to see here. Be prepared for anything. Ready to walk the surface?

SHANE: Check. Let's go, people.

ANEESA: Is anyone else nervous?

ORLANDO: There's no need to be nervous. We've detected no signs of life here.

ANEESA: Are you sure the heat sensor is working?

ORLANDO: Absolutely.

SHANE: Enough talking. Let's go complete the mission.

LUCY: I give the orders here. No more talking. We have a mission to complete.

SHANE: That's what I—

LUCY/ANEESA/ORLANDO: Shhh!

(LUCY, ANEESA, SHANE, and ORLANDO climb onto the surface of the planet.)

LUCY: *(Speaking quietly into a recording device.)* On the surface. Observe ice. No signs of life. Very quiet.

(Quiet beat while LUCY, ANEESA, SHANE, and ORLANDO look around.)

SHANE: I think I see something!

LUCY/ANEESA/ORLANDO: Shhh!

SHANE: (*Quieter.*) I think I see something!

ANEESA: What is it?

SHANE: I think it's—

ORLANDO: A palace! Made of ice!

LUCY: (*Speaking into her recording device.*) Correction. Potential signs of life. A palace in the distance.

ANEESA: Do you detect any signs of life on the sensor?

ORLANDO: None at all! Maybe it is broken.

LUCY: Perhaps everyone who lived in that palace has died.

SHANE: Maybe whatever killed them is still here somewhere.

ANEESA: I think I left something in the ship. Yeah. My, uh, lucky shrimp.

SHANE: You have a lucky shrimp?

ANEESA: Um, oh yeah. Definitely. I don't go anywhere without my lucky shrimp.

ORLANDO: Doesn't it smell bad? Seafood doesn't stay good for long.

ANEESA: Well, this is a very special shrimp, so if you'll excuse me—

LUCY: No one is going anywhere. We must stick together.

ANEESA: Must we?

LUCY: Of course we must.

ANEESA: Oh.

ORLANDO: Should we move closer?

SHANE: Let's storm the castle!

ORLANDO/LUCY/ANEESA: Shhh!

SHANE: *(In a tiny, high voice.)* Let's storm the castle!

LUCY: Let's take things one step at a time. We still don't know what we're dealing with here.

(TIP, PULL, PING, FLICK, and GIDDY enter quietly. They stand silently, observing the strangers.)

LUCY: **If there's one thing I've learned in my years of space travel, it's caution. Respect. Close observation of the environment.**

SHANE: That's three things!

LUCY: **OK, so I've learned three things. Before we leap into anything, we must get an idea of what's on this planet now and, perhaps, what used to be here. Get a sense of what's occurred in the past. If there has been some kind of war or extinction of life here, we need to know that. Otherwise, we could find ourselves dead as well. We must be smart about this. We must use all the science at our disposal.**

SHANE: You say the word "must" a lot.

LUCY: Sometimes you must use the word "must." For example, you must not interrupt me when I'm speaking, Shane. Let's gather some samples from the environment—dirt, leaves—anything we can find. The fate of the world could rest in our hands. Be prepared for danger, excitement, adventure, and perhaps . . . soil samples.

ORLANDO: There's no dirt.

ANEESA: There're no leaves.

SHANE: Just ice.

LUCY: Ice, then! Get samples of the ice!

ORLANDO: It will melt.

LUCY: Do it anyway!

SHANE: How come when she screams no one tells her to shhh?

ANEESA/ORLANDO/LUCY: Shhh!

(LUCY, ANEESA, and ORLANDO collect samples of ice while SHANE wanders off, sulking.)

SHANE: *(Muttering to himself.)* "Shhh, Shane. You're too loud, Shane. Shane, stop eating all the potato chips, we have only one bag left for the next five million light years." Everyone's bossy. Think they're the boss of me. They're not! I'm the boss of me. I know as much as them. I don't need them. Maybe

I'll just live here on my own. Seems nice enough. I can live in that palace. It would be cool living in an ice palace. And it would be all mine. I wouldn't let them visit. I can hear them begging, "Oh, Shane, your ice palace is so cool, can't we please visit?" And I'll be like, "No, this is my ice palace, losers! Get your own!" And they'll cry like babies 'cause that's what they are. "Shane, we miss you on board the ship. Come back with us, please? No one else can burp the alphabet. It's so boring without you!" I'm the real leader around here, and they'll be sorry when I go!

(SHANE bumps into TIP.)

TIP: Leader?

SHANE: Yes.

(TIP, PULL, PING, FLICK, and GIDDY gather around SHANE.)

SHANE: I mean no! I'm not the leader. Who are you? Go away! I'm just—I just burp a lot! You don't want me.

PULL: Leader! You come with us.

SHANE: You've got this all wrong.

PING: Leader, you come with us.

SHANE: This is all a big misunderstanding.

FLICK: Come with us, Leader.

SHANE: See that girl over there? The bossy one? She's the one you want.

GIDDY: Come to the palace with us, Leader.

SHANE: The palace?

TIP: The Queen will want to see you.

SHANE: Queen?

PULL: Do you always repeat?

SHANE: Repeat? Repeat what?

FLICK: This way, Leader.

SHANE: Wait. Hey, you guys!

ORLANDO/LUCY/ANEESA: Shhh!

SHANE: OK, fine. Let's go to the palace. That'll show them.

Scene 2: The Teen Queen

SHANE: So, you've got a Queen, huh? Is she bossy?

PING: What is "bossy"?

SHANE: Bossy is when you get told what to do all the time. I get told what to do *all* the time. I mean, even though I'm the leader! Can you believe it? I don't get any respect. There is a lot I know. You have no idea. And I do all the really hard work, really scientific stuff, you wouldn't even understand it, I swear, but still I don't get respect. It's wrong. It's outrageous! I bet your Queen doesn't get any of that stuff from you guys. You seem properly respectful. I mean, look at you, all shuffling along together, working as a team . . . that's what a leader wants! People who just do their job and don't whine about it. I mean . . . um . . . This isn't whining! I don't whine. I'm a leader! I *discuss*. This doesn't count as whining. I'm totally not a whiner. I hate whining. I just have a lot of complaints, that's all. It's totally different. You see what I mean, right? *(Beat.)* Anyway, your Queen, is she old?

GIDDY: Older than Giddy.

SHANE: What's Giddy?

(TIP, PULL, PING, and FLICK point to GIDDY.)

SHANE: Oh. Is the Queen pretty?

FLICK: The Queen is the Queen.

TIP: You talk too much, Leader.

PULL: You must be respectful of the Queen.

SHANE: Oh, yeah. I've got loads of respect. But I'm a leader, too, you know. I hope your Queen has some respect for me.

GIDDY: The Queen is always respectful.

FLICK: She is the Queen!

SHANE: How come you can't be picked up on our sensors?

TIP: Your sensors?

SHANE: Yeah. Our heat sensors.

(At the word "heat," TIP, PULL, PING, FLICK, and GIDDY flinch and shudder.)

PING: We do not like your "heat."

PULL: We have no need for it!

TIP: We live in ice.

FLICK: Duh.

GIDDY: Do you see now?

SHANE: Sure, sure. That makes sense.

TIP: Now, the Queen will arrive any moment.

SHANE: Excellent.

(SHANE, TIP, PULL, PING, FLICK, and GIDDY wait.)

SHANE: So, your Queen, is she going to be happy to see me?

GIDDY: Oh, yes!

SHANE: OK. Good.

(After another beat, the QUEEN enters.)

QUEEN: What is it? I was sleeping!

TIP: Queen, we bring you an alien!

SHANE: I'm not an alien. You're the alien!

PULL: Respect, human!

SHANE: I'm just saying . . .

QUEEN: Shut up already. Come here.

SHANE: You can't boss me around. They didn't tell you yet, but I'm a leader.

QUEEN: Uh-huh. Come here already.

(SHANE obeys. The QUEEN walks a big, slow circle around him, observing him.)

GIDDY: We have done well?

(Beat.)

QUEEN: You have done well.

PING: Take him to the kitchen?

SHANE: I am so hungry. That would be great. What do
you eat around here anyway?

QUEEN: Leader.

SHANE: Yes?

QUEEN: Leader.

SHANE: Yes?

QUEEN: Leader.

SHANE: Ye—

FLICK: That's what we eat.

SHANE: Huh? Oh. My. God! But—but—I'm not really the
leader! I was pretending! The girl, that bossy girl who's
always like, "Shane, you do this! Shane, you do that!
Shane, be quiet!"

PULL: Be quiet.

SHANE: She's the leader! She's the one you want!

QUEEN: You will do very well. Take him away.

SHANE: What are you going to do to me? Don't I at least
deserve to know that?

QUEEN: Very well. **My chefs will prepare you as our**

main course at our feast tonight. First, you will be tenderized with a mallet. You appear already to be somewhat tenderized as your flesh is soft and flabby—

SHANE: It is not! I just like potato chips!

TIP: Silence!

QUEEN: —but I like my meat tender so the chefs will beat you anyway. Once that process is done, the chefs will marinade you in a sauce. A spicy sauce for you. It goes with your personality. A mild sauce wouldn't suit you.

SHANE: Thank you.

QUEEN: Lastly, the chefs will separate the various delicacies from your body—heart, eyes, and so on. You will be served on various silver platters and passed out to my guests and me. I'd appreciate it if you wouldn't be bitter about all this because it ruins the meal. I don't like bitter meat. You understand, don't you? It would ruin a perfectly nice meal.

SHANE: Of course. Makes perfect sense.

QUEEN: You are very agreeable. I respect that in a leader.

SHANE: Thank you.

QUEEN: I think I will very much like you.

SHANE: Queen, you're making me blush.

QUEEN: Then I will let you go to the kitchen now.

SHANE: I appreciate that. See you later, then.

QUEEN: Yes. Later.

(SHANE begins to exit with TIP, PULL, PING, FLICK, and GIDDY.)

QUEEN: Oh, Tip?

TIP: Yes, Queen?

QUEEN: A spicy sauce. Be sure to tell the chefs.

TIP: Very well.

(SHANE, TIP, PULL, PING, FLICK, and GIDDY exit. There's a long beat while the QUEEN sits on her throne and pulls out a knife and fork. SHANE enters suddenly in a panic.)

SHANE: Wait just one minute! You're going to eat me?

QUEEN: I believe I made that clear.

SHANE: But you never mentioned any cooking of the meat.

QUEEN: We like our meat raw. It's a cultural thing. Is that a problem?

SHANE: No, no. To each her own, I guess. OK.

(SHANE exits. Another long beat as the QUEEN looks at her reflection in the knife. SHANE reenters suddenly.)

SHANE: Wait! You're going to eat me?

QUEEN: Which part of this don't you understand? We'll tenderize you, marinade you, pull you apart, and serve you to my guests as the main course at a feast.

SHANE: I don't think I like that.

QUEEN: Well, too bad. I'm the Queen.

SHANE: And I'm a Leader!

QUEEN: I thought you weren't.

SHANE: Well, maybe I am!

QUEEN: Mmm, Leader.

SHANE: No, no! I'm not a leader.

QUEEN: Are you or aren't you?

SHANE: I'm not!

(The QUEEN considers this information for a moment.)

QUEEN: You're not just saying that so you can live, are you?

SHANE: Well, that's not the only reason I'm saying it. It's true!

QUEEN: Hmmm. Well, you still look juicy and fit for a meal.

SHANE: There's nothing fit about me! You were right! I'm lazy and disgusting and have terrible hygiene.

QUEEN: Hmmm. Tip!

(TIP enters.)

TIP: Yes, Queen?

QUEEN: Be sure to scrub him thoroughly clean before tenderizing him.

TIP: Yes, Queen.

QUEEN: Take him away.

SHANE: Wait!

(LUCY, ANEESA, and ORLANDO enter.)

LUCY: Wait!

(PULL, PING, FLICK, and GIDDY enter to guard the QUEEN.)

QUEEN: Who are these aliens?

LUCY: We came on your planet to observe its life forms. We mean no harm. However, we'd like to get our comrade back. Have you seen him? Big mouth, difficult, a little bit dim . . .

QUEEN: I have seen him, but he is mine now.

ORLANDO: Let him go!

FLICK: Are you threatening the Queen?

ORLANDO: No, we just want Shane back.

QUEEN: But why? He is difficult, as you say.

ANEESA: But he's one of us, so we have a duty—

QUEEN: He is lazy and stupid, yes?

ANEESA: Well . . . yes.

QUEEN: Why don't you stay for our feast and we can talk it over.

ORLANDO: We are pretty hungry.

ANEESA: What do you think, Lucy?

QUEEN: Lucy? You are the leader then?

LUCY: Yes. I am the leader.

PING: Mmm.

LUCY: What was that?

QUEEN: What Ping means to say is mmmarvelous! A leader in our midst!

LUCY: Thank you.

QUEEN: Let the feast begin!

TALK BACK!

1. Do you prefer to be a leader or a follower?

2. What are the qualities needed to be a leader?

3. Do you know of any cultures that have very different and interesting customs from ours?

4. What do you think might happen next in the story (if there was a Scene 3)?

5. What qualities do explorers and pioneers need to have?

6. Are there advantages to pretending you're something you're not?

THE NANNY

3F, 1M

WHO

FEMALES MALES
June Parker
Mom
Nanny

WHERE At home.

WHEN Present day.

June, Parker, Mom: Think about how you act with your actual family. See if you can use this information when you interact with your fictional family. Nanny: Remember that Nanny has to seem nice to the Mom and not totally evil at all times.

Think of a regular, everyday problem and make it into a horror story. For example, think of a reason why it would be *terrible* to take a bath.

Scene 1: Rebellion

JUNE: I hope she'll be nice like Mary Poppins.

PARKER: I am not going to sing. But it would be great if she was magic.

JUNE: And if she had a bag that could hold endless amounts of stuff.

PARKER: What?

JUNE: Like Mary Poppins. She took a coat rack out of her handbag.

PARKER: Whatever. Who cares about that? Anyway, it's impossible.

JUNE: You were saying you wish she was magic. How is that different?

PARKER: Magic is real, stupid.

MOM: Kids! This is why we need a nanny. You fight day and night. I just can't take it.

PARKER: Mom, I don't get why we need a nanny. We're not that bad.

JUNE: And we're not babies. We're practically adults!

MOM: I have to go back to work. And someone's got to watch you.

JUNE: No one has to watch us!

PARKER: You can leave us on our own.

MOM: No way. If this is how you behave when I'm here, then I definitely couldn't leave you on your own. It's for your own safety.

PARKER: This is stupid. It's for babies.

MOM: Maybe if you didn't act like a baby . . .

JUNE: Ha-ha!

MOM: Quiet, June! She'll be here any minute. I want you two to be on your best behavior for her.

PARKER: Why? Shouldn't she be trying to impress us, not the other way around?

MOM: Parker . . . behave yourself!

PARKER: Aw, Mom.

JUNE: You got burned by Mom a second time!

MOM: June!

(*The doorbell rings.*)

MOM: Last warning, kids. Behave.

(MOM *exits to answer the door.*)

JUNE: If she looks like Mrs. Doubtfire should we try to rip her wig off?

PARKER: It would be great to scare her away.

JUNE: Mom would kill us. Then she'd probably just get us another nanny.

PARKER: But we'd be dead!

JUNE: You know what I mean.

(The NANNY enters with MOM.)

MOM: I'll leave all of you to get acquainted. Mathilda, these are my children, Parker and June.

PARKER: *(To JUNE.)* Mathilda!

JUNE: Shhh!

NANNY: You can call me Nanny, children. They are lovely, Mrs. Silver.

MOM: Yes, well . . . yes, they are. Very well behaved, aren't you, children?

JUNE: Sure, Mom.

PARKER: You bet.

(MOM exits.)

NANNY: Dear, lovely children. We are going to get along just fine.

JUNE: Sure.

PARKER: You bet.

NANNY: Just as long as you do everything I say.

JUNE: Oh . . .

PARKER: Well . . .

NANNY: Do we understand each other?

JUNE: I guess.

PARKER: Depends on what you ask us to do.

NANNY: You will do what I say, young man. It will be for your own good!

(MOM enters.)

MOM: How's everything going so far? Getting acquainted?

JUNE: Mom?

NANNY: Yes, we understand each other perfectly, don't we, June?

JUNE: Well, actually, Mom—

PARKER: Do we have to do *everything* she says?

MOM: Yes, of course. She's like your mom when I'm at work. You need to obey and respect Nanny Mathilda.

JUNE: What—what if—

PARKER: What if we don't want to? She's not really in charge of us.

MOM: Of course she is. Now stop being argumentative. Be nice to Nanny. Nanny, would you like a cup of tea?

NANNY: I'd love that, dear.

(MOM exits.)

NANNY: Well, I hope that clears things up.

PARKER: I still don't think I have to do *everything* you say.

NANNY: You heard your mother, son.

JUNE: Parker, lay off. Mom's right. Besides, you wouldn't ask us to do anything horrible, would you? Just regular stuff like clean our rooms and do our homework, right?

NANNY: But of course.

PARKER: I hate that stuff.

NANNY: Then we are going to have a problem, young man.

JUNE: Come on, Park. Try to be good. Let's not get off on the wrong foot.

PARKER: Well, OK. But I still don't know about this "do everything I say" stuff.

NANNY: My dear, what in the world must be in your head? I think you're frightened of me.

PARKER: I'm not scared of anything.

NANNY: You're not scared of anything at all?

PARKER: No.

NANNY: We shall see.

JUNE: What do you—
   (MOM re-enters.)

MOM: Here's your tea, Nanny Mathilda.

NANNY: Thank you, dear.

MOM: Everyone getting along?

NANNY: They're just a little nervous. I'm a stranger, aren't I? But your mother chose me to take care of you because I have excellent credentials and I'm the right person for the job.

JUNE: But Mom . . .

MOM: Yes, June?

JUNE: Do we really need a nanny? What if we absolutely, positively promise to be good?

PARKER: What if she's a man?

MOM: Parker! You stop this right now! I need you to behave yourself! This is very important to me. I need to return to work, and I need to know that you kids are safe while I'm gone.

PARKER: But Mom—

MOM: Parker, please!

JUNE: Fine, Mom. We'll be good.

NANNY: They'll be good, Mrs. Silver.

MOM: I'm so sorry, Nanny.

NANNY: Don't worry yourself, child. I'm just a new face to them. It's natural that they'd be nervous.

MOM: Well, I apologize for their behavior. It won't happen again, will it?

JUNE: No, Mom.

PARKER: No, Mom.

MOM: OK. Well. I'll be going now.

NANNY: Yes, you be on your way. Everything is fine here.

MOM: Thank you, Nanny.

(MOM *exits.*)

NANNY: Now where were we? Oh yes. Parker, I think Nanny needs to have her feet rubbed and her toenails clipped.

PARKER: No way!

NANNY: I think you will.

PARKER: I think I won't.

NANNY: I think if you don't, I will tell your mother that you cheated on a test.

PARKER: But I didn't!

NANNY: Whom is she going to believe? "Mrs. Silver, Parker has just admitted to me something quite terrible . . . "

PARKER: You wouldn't!

NANNY: Try me.

JUNE: Nanny, why are you being so cruel? Aren't you supposed to like kids? We haven't really done anything at all to you. OK, we have a little bit of an attitude, but can't you understand that? We don't want a nanny. We don't think we need a nanny. I mean, we're pretty old. I can manage to get my homework done when no one's reminding me. It seems really silly to be treated like a baby like this. We can work the microwave, so we can eat. There's really nothing we can't do on our own. We're kids, but we're not *kids*, know what I mean? So maybe we can call a truce, find some way to get along so we don't feel like we're two years old and you don't have to do very much. What do you think?

NANNY: While Parker is clipping my toenails, you can tweeze the hairs out of my moles.

PARKER: No way! You lose, old lady. No way are we doing this stuff for you. You can tell my mom anything you want. We're her kids; she'll believe us, not you. You're an old creep. Does this really work at other people's houses? I'm guessing it doesn't or you wouldn't be working for us now. I bet you got fired. I bet you've never worked as a nanny before. You're a horrible old witch, and I'm not scared of you! You're nothing. And you can't make me, or my sister, do anything. When I tell my mother what you asked us to do, she'll be furious. You'd better start running now because the police will be after you in no time, witch. Tell you what, I'll give you a head start, and you can maybe just do a leisurely jog because I don't want to see your butt jiggling. But make no mistake. You're through, lady.

Scene 2: Revenge

PARKER: You can't hold us prisoner like this! Where did you get these bars from anyway?

NANNY: I stashed them in my trunk. Clever, eh?

JUNE: You'll never get away with this. Our mother will be coming home.

NANNY: She'll be coming home to a clean and tidy house and well-behaved children. She won't complain about my methods.

PARKER: She will when we tell her about them!

NANNY: Parker, when will you learn? You won't tell her about my disciplinary methods. If you do, I will tell her something about you that she won't like at all. And your mother will believe me, not you. I am sure of it.

JUNE: Our mother loves us.

NANNY: Your mother loves you. How sweet. But she doesn't love your behavior. She doesn't love being with you. Why do you think she's run away to work? To get away from you. That's why I'm here. So stop arguing and fighting and start doing what I tell you. I'll break you sooner or later, and it's much easier for everyone if it's sooner.

JUNE: This isn't fair!

NANNY: Oh, children. Tell you what I'll do. To make it up to you, I'll feed you both lots and lots of cupcakes. I'll be back in a jiffy. See, I'm not such a monster, am

I? Now make those floors shine so I can see my pretty face in them!

(NANNY *exits*.)

PARKER: Pretty face? I've seen prettier faces on orangutans.

JUNE: I'm so hungry, Park; I've cleaned the whole house.

PARKER: And the garage.

JUNE: And weeded the garden.

PARKER: And rubbed Nanny's feet.

JUNE: And tweezed her hairy moles.

PARKER: And clipped her toenails.

JUNE: And massaged the hump on her back.

PARKER: And polished her wand.

JUNE: And . . . wait! What did you say?

PARKER: Polished her wand.

JUNE: Do you think she could be . . .

PARKER: What, a witch? Well, yeah!

JUNE: So how are we going to get out of this?

PARKER: You heard her. We can't. Mom *will* believe her.

JUNE: No, she wouldn't.

PARKER: Sure she would!

JUNE: What can we do?

PARKER: Nothing.

JUNE: We haven't even done our homework yet! We'll have to stay up all night!

PARKER: If we're alive. I bet those cupcakes are poisoned.

JUNE: Why would she poison us?

PARKER: 'Cause she's mean and evil.

JUNE: What if she's trying to fatten us up and eat us? Like Hansel and Gretel?

PARKER: Well, that'll take a while at least.

JUNE: I don't want to spend another day like this, Parker. We have to think of something.

PARKER: Hansel and Gretel pushed the witch in the oven.

JUNE: She's way bigger than our oven.

PARKER: I've got an idea—

(NANNY enters.)

JUNE: What is it?

PARKER: Shhh!

NANNY: Here are those cupcakes!

PARKER: Nanny?

NANNY: Yes, horrible, bad boy?

PARKER: Your little stick—

NANNY: My wand?

PARKER: Yes. I don't think I shined it up enough. I don't want to make you mad.

NANNY: That's better. I'm glad you're coming over to my way of thinking.

PARKER: Well, I see your point.

JUNE: Parker!

NANNY: My wand looks very shiny, though. I think it's fine.

PARKER: I see a spot I missed.

NANNY: I don't.

PARKER: OK. I admit it. I spit on it. I want to clean it off again.

NANNY: You naughty boy! Very well, then. Clean it well this time or I will be very, very cross with you.

PARKER: Yes, Nanny.

(NANNY passes PARKER her wand.)

PARKER: *(Waving the wand at NANNY.)* Cluck like a chicken!

(NANNY clucks like a chicken.)

PARKER: *(Waving the wand at NANNY.)* Act like an elephant!

(NANNY acts like an elephant.)

PARKER: *(Waving the wand at NANNY.)* Sound like a giraffe!

(NANNY looks at PARKER, confused.)

PARKER: *(Waving the wand at NANNY.)* You're a pig!

(NANNY gets down on her hands and knees and acts like a pig.)

JUNE: Parker, you're a genius!

PARKER: *(Waving the wand.)* Get these bars away!

(NANNY throws the bars to the floor.)

JUNE: Thank you, Parker! You're the bravest, smartest, truest brother there ever was. I didn't think I'd ever say that. I certainly didn't think I'd ever mean it! But I'm sorry for all the times when we fought. You really are decent most of the time. I don't hate you. I still find you annoying, but I don't hate you. I'm glad you're my brother. I know that's gross to say, but it's true. I'm so proud of you for getting us out of this mess. But what are we going to do with the witch now that you've turned her into a pig? And what will we say to Mom? Wait—I know! We could just send her away with the wand and tell Mom she quit, right? Mom will be mad at us, but then she'll see how clean the house is, and she'll forgive us! Then we'll live happily ever after! Except for the witch, of course

PARKER: We can tell her we cleaned the house *after* Nanny left to make it up to her!

JUNE: Sure! That's great.

PARKER: You're not so terrible either. I don't wanna get all mushy or anything, though.

JUNE: I understand.

PARKER: So let's get rid of Nanny once and for all. *(Waving the wand at NANNY.)* Get outta here forever!

(NANNY crawls in a piglike way off the stage.)

PARKER: Free at last! Now I'm going to have one of these cupcakes!

JUNE: Parker, don't!

(PARKER eats a cupcake.)

PARKER: It actually tastes good. Is anything happening to me? Am I turning into anything?

JUNE: No.

PARKER: The witch's cupcakes are really delicious! You should try one, June. Don't be afraid; they're not poisoned. I wonder why she made them? *(Beat.)* I just had a really awful thought. What if she was just trying to make us be good kids? What if she just wanted us to clean the house? Sure she put us behind bars for a while and threatened us and made us clip her toenails—

JUNE: And tweeze the hairs from her moles!

PARKER: —but other than that, she just acted like a parent. Parents can be pretty terrible, can't they! I mean, they make us do chores and stuff! It's not right! We should be free to do anything we want. Maybe *all* adults are witches. Maybe we're prisoners all the time only we're too dumb to know it. *(Beat.)* Then again, I don't think Mom has any special powers, and she never made us massage her hunchback or anything. She's just a mom. Most of the time it's pretty OK being here. Hey—these cupcakes are delicious, June! If witches make cupcakes this good, maybe I shouldn't complain!

JUNE: But adults also teach us and feed us and are nice to us a lot, too. And we do act like brats sometimes. That's why Nanny's threats worked, because we knew they were true.

PARKER: I don't know. Maybe Mom would have believed us and not her. I mean, we are her kids.

JUNE: Yeah, but Nanny was an adult.

PARKER: That's not right. Adults should believe us.

JUNE: I don't know. It's all very confusing.

PARKER: Have a cupcake.

JUNE: OK.

(PARKER walks over to JUNE to give her a cupcake. His feet are now extremely hairy.)

JUNE: Parker, look! They *were* magic cupcakes!

(Beat.)

PARKER: Oh well. They are really good, June. Seriously. It's worth it.

JUNE: OK!

TALK BACK!

1. What annoying things do your parents do and what are their reasons for doing them? Are they right or wrong?

2. Are chores necessary? Why or why not? What can you learn from doing chores, if anything?

3. What chore seems most like a punishment to you?

4. If you were in danger, who would you try to protect?

5. Is it good or bad to be suspicious of adults?

6. Do you ever feel unheard because you're a kid? Why?

7. If you told adults one thing about kids you think they should know, what would it be?

BEES!

3F, 4M

WHO

FEMALES	MALES
Andrea	Brian
Lydia	Anthony
Jolie	Matt
	Neil

WHERE Scene 1: Behind an auditorium; Scene 2: Outside.

WHEN Present day.

🎭 Scene 1: Make the brainy kids as quirky and super-smart as you'd like, but don't make fun of them. Act like you think they really would.
Scene 2: Read the scene carefully and see what you can figure out about your character from the lines they say and what's said about him or her.

✎ In Scene 2, I used a monologue I previously wrote for *The Ultimate Monologue Book for Middle School Actors, Volume 1*. Try using a monologue from another source and building your own unique scene around it.

Pronunciation Key for Scene 1

[1] Chlorophyll: KLOR-uh-fil

[2] Photosynthetic: fo-to-sin-THEH-tik

[3] Chiaroscurist: kee-are-uh-SKUR-ist

[4] Prospicience: pro-SPISH-ee-ens

[5] Quokka: KWAH-kuh

[6] Quodlibet: KWAHD-li-bet

Scene 1: Queen Bee

ANDREA: I can't do this! I can't do this! I don't know anyone or anything. I can't remember my name. I want to go home. I can't take this!

BRIAN: Snap out of it! We've been practicing for this since birth. You'll be fine. Spell chlorophyll.[1]

ANDREA: That's an easy one. You know it's an easy one!

BRIAN: So spell it.

ANDREA: C-H-L-O-R-O-P-H-Y-L-L. Wait! Is this a trick? You did say chlorophyll, right? As in the green photosynthetic[2] pigment found chiefly in the chloroplasts of plants?

BRIAN: Well, duh. So you got it right!

ANDREA: Give me a hard one.

BRIAN: I'm not sure you can handle it.

ANDREA: I can handle it! Give it to me!

BRIAN: Chiaroscurist.[3]

ANDREA: The National Spelling Bee final word in 1998. Simple. Too obvious. But I'll spell it anyway. C-H-I-A-R-O-S-C-U-R-I-S-T.

BRIAN: You're fine. So stop worrying.

ANDREA: But I need to win!

BRIAN: I'm going to win. So you can stop worrying.

(LYDIA enters.)

LYDIA: I'm afraid I'm going to win, kids.

ANDREA: Oh my God, Lydia Hortzhoffer, winner of last year's National Spelling Bee! Oh my God, I love it when you spell. You're, like, amazing to watch. I remember when you were spelling prospicience[4]—

LYDIA: P-R-O-S-P-I-C-I-E-N-C-E. Meaning foresight.

ANDREA: —and there was this kid before you who used an extra "e"—

LYDIA: Please, like there should be another "e" in prospicience.

ANDREA: I know! And so, he was crying while you were trying to spell, and I was thinking, "She can't do it! There are too many distractions! She's getting confused!"

LYDIA: It was all an act.

ANDREA: And then you got it right and I was like, "Oh my God, she got it right!" Then that kid started crying even more—

LYDIA: It's the pressure. You have to be able to handle the pressure.

ANDREA: And I was like, "I'm going to *be* Lydia Hortzhoffer next year."

LYDIA: You can't be me. I'm me.

ANDREA: Well, I didn't mean it. I just mean, well . . . I was impressed.

LYDIA: You love me. You want to be me.

ANDREA: No, I don't!

BRIAN: Well, Lydia, I'm afraid no one wins twice in a row.

LYDIA: Well, there's no one else like me. I'm an original. I'm the quintessential speller.

BRIAN: You're a quokka.[5]

LYDIA: A reddish-brown short-tailed wallaby?

BRIAN: You heard me. Need me to spell it?

ANDREA: Come on, you guys. Who's the best speller is a quodlibet[6] we could argue about all day.

LYDIA: Is not. We'll find out soon enough.

BRIAN: We need to get in place. It's about to start.

ANDREA: **What if I suddenly get sick?**

LYDIA: This is going to be televised on national television.

BRIAN: Televised implies that it's going to be on television. That was redundant.

ANDREA: **I don't want to be a laughingstock. A fool. An ignoramus. A buffoon. A harebrain. A nincom-**

poop. A horse's behind. A dingaling. A simpleton. An imbecile—

BRIAN: Andrea, stop! Control yourself!

ANDREA: **I don't want to be any of those things on TV. I've seen those people. They cry. I don't want to cry! I don't know if I'm strong enough for this. I know I'm smart enough. I can spell anything. But with the pressure on, I don't know. I don't want pity. I don't want parents saying, "Awww." I hate the "awww." It's the worst thing ever. You know you're a pathetic neonate then. "Neonate[7]: N-E-O-N-A-T-E. A newborn child." I can do this. I find spelling relaxing. I do! I find people staring at me terrifying, but I find spelling relaxing. I can do this. I can do this. I am a virtuoso: V-I-R-T-U-O-S-O.**

BRIAN: That's right, Andrea. You can do this.

LYDIA: Why are you so nice to her?

BRIAN: She's my friend.

LYDIA: She's your competition.

BRIAN: And she's my friend.

LYDIA: That doesn't make any sense.

BRIAN: Sure it does. I don't have to hate her to compete against her.

LYDIA: Sure you do. What if it comes down to you or her?

ANDREA: I hope you win.

BRIAN: I hope we both win.

LYDIA: You can't both win. Who do you really want to win? I bet *you* want to win yourself.

BRIAN: Well, maybe I do. And I bet deep down Andrea wants to win, too.

ANDREA: No, I don't. **I don't want my picture in the papers.**

BRIAN: Sure you do.

ANDREA: No, actually. **I'm terrified of having my picture taken.**

BRIAN: Seriously? It's just a little flash. It's not going to hurt you.

ANDREA: It's not that. **It's just that I have no control over my facial expressions, it seems. I always look, well, drunk.**

BRIAN: But you're not.

ANDREA: Of course not. **It's just that my face seems to go crazy when someone says, "Say cheese!" I start to think, "Why not please? Why do I have to smile anyway? Plus, I don't like cheese; I'm lactose intolerant. I hope I don't look stupid." And somehow between all these thoughts, I get a very stupid and embarrassing look on my face. So I would rather not have my picture in the paper. I prefer to be mysterious than embarrassed.**

BRIAN: Yeah, but don't you want to tell people forever that you were the National Spelling Bee winner?

LYDIA: And aren't your parents going to kill you if you blow it?

ANDREA: Maybe. **My parents really want this for me. They want me to succeed. I wonder sometimes if it would be easier if I failed or succeeded. If I fail, maybe they'll give me a break and I can watch TV or play a video game every once in a while. And if I succeed, they'll be so proud—I know they do this because they want the best for me. Why is nothing easy?**

BRIAN: I know. But you're right. Sometimes it would be nice just to be a dumb, old kid.

LYDIA: "Old kid" is an oxymoron. The words contradict each other.

BRIAN: Yeah? So?

LYDIA: So? I just thought you should know.

BRIAN: I know. But that's just it! Wouldn't it be nice if I didn't know and I could just say whatever popped into my head? After all, we're only kids. We don't need all this pressure.

LYDIA: You don't want to win! You're going to lose, lose, lose!

BRIAN: Whatever. I'm going to mop the floor with you.

LYDIA: If it comes down to you or her, you'll feel bad for her and you'll lose. See? Friends just make you weak.

BRIAN: That is so sad.

LYDIA: It's the truth! You don't want to face it.

BRIAN: Well, I'd rather have friends than be angry and alone all the time.

LYDIA: I guess that's the difference between you and me.

BRIAN: I guess so.

ANDREA: I forget how to spell "spell"!

BRIAN: You're going to be fine, Andrea.

LYDIA: You're going to lose.

BRIAN: *(To LYDIA.)* You're going to go away now. And you're going to be fine, Andrea. Don't let her get to you. You can spell anything.

ANDREA: Thanks, Brian. Thanks a lot.

LYDIA: Good luck. Don't wet your pants or anything.

BRIAN: Ditto.

Scene 2: Two Bees or Not Two Bees

NEIL: Guys, I'm really sorry. There was this bee in my eye. Right in my eye! And I couldn't see the ball. I thought it would sting me in the eye! You can imagine. I could be blind now. But I smacked that bee. I think I killed it. I'm OK now. Is anybody listening? Guys, really, I'm sorry I let you down. It was just that bee—

JOLIE: You were daydreaming. That's why you missed the ball.

NEIL: I wasn't daydreaming! I was paying attention! Ready to go! Ready for action! And then that bee—

MATT: Shut up, Neil.

NEIL: I won't shut up! You gotta understand that I was in danger.

ANTHONY: You let us down. You lost us the game.

NEIL: No, I didn't!

JOLIE: Yes, you did.

NEIL: Well, I didn't mean to.

MATT: But you did.

ANTHONY: Thanks a lot.

NEIL: Well, no one actually hits balls into the outfield usually! That's why I'm *in* the outfield, stupids!

Everyone knows the outfield never has to do anything. Can I help it if some baseball genius—

MATT: There's no such thing as a baseball genius.

NEIL: Well, if some really good kid baseball player hits the ball into the outfield?

JOLIE: You can't help what he does, but you can help what you do.

NEIL: OK, fine. I stink! Is that what you want to hear? I stink!

ANTHONY: Yeah, you do. Tell us something we don't know.

(JOLIE, MATT, and ANTHONY exit.)

NEIL: Stupid jerks. I can't help that a baseball came at me at the same time a bee did and that I can't even play baseball really. Who can catch a fly ball? I hate sports. I hate everyone. Stupid jerks.

(Beat. JOLIE, MATT, and ANTHONY reenter, running and swatting their arms madly.)

MATT: Beeeeees!

NEIL: What?

ANTHONY: Attacking!

NEIL: Stop it. You're not funny.

JOLIE: Not trying to be funny!

MATT: Trying to escape the bees!

NEIL: Seriously. Stop.

ANTHONY: Help!

(JOLIE, MATT, and ANTHONY roll on the ground.)

MATT: Oh thank God!

JOLIE: Free at last!

ANTHONY: I thought we were goners!

(JOLIE, MATT, and ANTHONY become still and act normal again.)

NEIL: Very funny.

JOLIE: What?

NEIL: The bee thing.

MATT: I've never been attacked like that before.

ANTHONY: Those were mad bees. Crazy!

JOLIE: Killer bees.

MATT: We're lucky to be alive.

(Beat.)

NEIL: Well ha, ha, ha. I hope you had fun. You made your point. I'm a liar. I'm a loser. I made up the bee thing. Happy now? I'm just a terrible, terrible baseball player who can't even catch a ball. Worse than that, I can't even play attention. Truth is, I don't even like baseball. It's stupid. And baseball players, even when they're professional, don't even look like athletes. It's pathetic. They look like my dad. So why is this sport such a big deal? It's stupid. We're trying to hit a little ball then run around in circles. How stupid is that when you think about it? It's sad. Isn't there something better we could do with our time? Of course! But other kids and my dad expect me to do this and do it well. So I try. And this is what happens. I stink. And I get made fun of for even trying. This is just great. I don't know why I even bother. And now I'm going to be forced to keep going with all this even though all you guys hate me, *plus* I bet my dad will make me practice even *more* in the backyard on the weekends. This is horrible. This is like hell. Only instead of there being flames and devils with big forks, we have baseball. Which is even worse. I'd rather get my eye poked with a fork instead of this. This is not even funny.

ANTHONY: Who's being funny?

JOLIE: What are you talking about?

NEIL: I'm talking about baseball.

JOLIE: I got that, but what are you talking about?

NEIL: Are you going to make me spell it out for you? I stink. I S-T-I-N-K. And, fine, I lied about the bee thing. I L-I-E-D. There. Happy now?

ANTHONY: Dude, we were totally just attacked by bees.

MATT: Are you making a joke or something? 'Cause I don't get it.

JOLIE: We believe you. You can stop now.

MATT: It's scary and awful to be attacked by bees. I would have missed a fly ball, too.

ANTHONY: I can't believe how calm you were when they attacked you, Neil.

MATT: Yeah, you were pretty amazing.

JOLIE: How did you do it?

NEIL: How did I do it?

JOLIE: Yeah!

(Beat.)

NEIL: Well, it took a lot of concentration.

ANTHONY: Amazing.

NEIL: I *wanted* to catch the ball and win the game.

MATT: Oh my God.

NEIL: Right. So I thought maybe if I averted my eyes from the field and turned away from the bees, I might stand a better chance.

ANTHONY: Of course! So you faced away from the incoming ball.

MATT: It makes perfect sense now!

NEIL: I was looking out of the corner of my eye.

JOLIE: So it just *looked* like you weren't looking.

MATT: Brilliant!

NEIL: I just couldn't let those bees get my eyeballs. I was going to need them if there was any chance of catching that ball.

JOLIE: It's so tragic. That ball was yours.

NEIL: I know. I really thought I could do it. I just had to try to keep track of the ball and the attacking bees at the same time.

ANTHONY: That must have been hard.

NEIL: Hard? Please. I'm lucky to be alive.

JOLIE: Shhh!

NEIL: What?

JOLIE: I think . . .

MATT: I hear . . .

ANTHONY: Bees!

NEIL: Aaaaaah!

   (NEIL runs away.)

ANTHONY: That kid is seriously weird.

MATT: Did he really think we'd fall for that?

JOLIE: I do feel a little sorry for him.

MATT: Well, yeah.

ANTHONY: Why?

JOLIE: Well, he really shouldn't be playing baseball.

MATT: He stinks.

ANTHONY: Did you see how that ball just plopped down *right* in front of him?

JOLIE: Pathetic.

MATT: Sad. But he's right about one thing. Nobody really expects the outfield to do anything.

ANTHONY: True . . . We should try to get that other guy on our team, the one who hit that ball into the outfield . . .

(JOLIE, ANTHONY, and MATT exit as they talk. NEIL reenters.)

NEIL: Guys? Where are you? I don't actually see the bees anymore. Maybe I scared them off. Want to go get some pizza? Guys?

TALK BACK!

1. What do you think of Andrea and Neil's predicaments?

2. Do you do any activities that you secretly hate because your parents want you to do it?

3. Is it guidance or cruelty when a parent forces you to try a new activity?

4. Are you good at saying no to authority figures? Why is this easy or hard for you? What's the right way to refuse to do something you don't want to do?

5. When should you quit something you hate and when should you "tough it out"?

6. When is it OK to be proud of your accomplishments, like Lydia, and when is it obnoxious?

7. Are you a competitive person? How?

8. Are sports or spelling natural talents or things you can learn? Is it fair to expect everyone to be good at these activities?

9. Which spelling rules don't make sense to you?

APPENDIX

CHARACTER QUESTIONNAIRE FOR ACTORS

Fill in the following questionnaire as if you are your character. Make up anything you don't know.

PART 1: The Facts

NAME:

AGE/BIRTHDATE:

HEIGHT:

WEIGHT:

HAIR COLOR:

EYE COLOR:

CITY/STATE/COUNTRY YOU LIVE IN:

GRADE*:

BROTHERS/SISTERS:

PARENTS:

UPBRINGING (strict, indifferent, permissive, etc.):

---

* If you are an adult, what educational level did you reach (college, medical school, high school, etc.)?

PART 2: Rate Yourself

On a scale of 1 to 10 (circle one: 10 = great, 1 = bad), rate your:

APPEARANCE	1 2 3 4 5 6 7 8 9 10
IQ	1 2 3 4 5 6 7 8 9 10
SENSE OF HUMOR	1 2 3 4 5 6 7 8 9 10
ATHLETICISM	1 2 3 4 5 6 7 8 9 10
ENTHUSIASM	1 2 3 4 5 6 7 8 9 10
CONFIDENCE	1 2 3 4 5 6 7 8 9 10
DETERMINATION	1 2 3 4 5 6 7 8 9 10
FRIENDLINESS	1 2 3 4 5 6 7 8 9 10
ARTISTICNESS	1 2 3 4 5 6 7 8 9 10

Do you like yourself?	YES	NO
Do you like your family?	YES	NO
Do you like the opposite sex?	YES	NO
Do you like most people you meet?	YES	NO

Which of the following are important to you and which are not? Circle one.

WEALTH	Important	Not Important
KNOWLEDGE	Important	Not Important
POWER	Important	Not Important
PEACE	Important	Not Important
POPULARITY	Important	Not Important
LIKABILITY	Important	Not Important
LOVE	Important	Not Important
SPIRITUALITY/RELIGION	Important	Not Important

PART 3: Favorites

List your favorites (be specific).

FOOD:

SONG:

BOOK:

MOVIE:

TV SHOW:

CITY:

SEASON:

COLOR:

PIECE OF CLOTHING:

SMELL:

ANIMAL:

SOUND:

SCHOOL SUBJECT:

PLACE:

PERSON (historical or living):

PART 4: Describe Yourself

Circle all words/phrases that apply to you:

SHY	OUTGOING
OUTDOOR TYPE	INDOOR TYPE
POSITIVE	NEGATIVE
PARTY PERSON	COUCH POTATO
HOMEBODY	LEADER
FOLLOWER	MOODY
CALM	SILLY
HAPPY	SAD
RELAXED	ENERGETIC
INTELLECTUAL	CLEVER
NEAT	MESSY
FUNNY	HONEST
SNEAKY	DISHONEST
OPEN-MINDED	JUDGMENTAL
CARING	CREATIVE
PRACTICAL	WILD
CAREFUL	WELL-LIKED
ARTISTIC	LAZY
OPINIONATED	IMAGINATIVE
REALISTIC	DRAMATIC
STREETWISE	TOLERANT
HARD-WORKING	SPONTANEOUS
STRONG	BRAVE
CURIOUS	QUIET
CHATTY	DARK
SUNNY	DISAPPOINTING
HOPEFUL	UNDERSTANDING
KIND	BORED
DIFFICULT	COMPLICATED
SWEET	POWERFUL
MACHO	ENTHUSIASTIC
GIRLY	INSECURE
LUCKY	PICKY
DISADVANTAGED	FRIENDLY
GOSSIPY	ANGRY
SECRETIVE	WISHY-WASHY
INDEPENDENT	GEEKY
WEAK	COOL
NURTURING	ANNOYING
REBELLIOUS	GOOD

PART 5: Truth/Dreams

If I die tomorrow, people will remember me as a:

One thing that really annoys me is:

My worst habit is:

I'm really scared of:

My parents think I'm:

When I grow up, I want to be*:

Superpower I'd most like to have:

The thing I'd most like to change about myself is:

My greatest talent is:

I'd most like to travel to:

Three professions I'd like to try:

The title for the story of my life would be:

* If your character is an adult, what is your character's job and does he or she enjoy it?

PLAYWRIGHT'S CHECKLIST

Does my play have:

☐ Conflict?

If everyone gets along, not much happens! It's important to have conflict in any play, comedy, or drama.

☐ Character development?

Do the characters change at all in the course of the play for better or worse? It's interesting to the audience to see some variety in character. We all act differently in different situations, so it makes sense for a character to become more complex when he or she is faced with conflicts.

☐ Plot twists?

What could be more exciting than being surprised by a plot twist you hadn't expected?

☐ Believable dialogue?

Even if the characters are strange and out-of-this-world, make sure the dialogue sounds something like the way people actually speak to one another. Any character voices you create must remain consistent throughout. For example, if a character is very intellectual and proper, having them say "I ain't gonna go" is going to seem very out of place.

☐ A strong sense of place and time?

Especially when you don't have a big set and costumes, it's important to make the play's setting clear.

☐ Characters you can relate to?

Every play has at least one character the audience can understand and sympathize with. A good way to create conflict is to put this "normal" character in the path of another character that is odd, otherworldly, or downright horrible!

SCENE ELEMENTS WORKSHEET

Answer these questions for each scene you do.

WHO: (Who are you?)

WHERE: (Where are you?)

WHEN: (Is this the past, present, or future? Day or night?)

WHY: (Why are you where you are?)

OBJECTIVE: (What do you want?)

ACTIONS: (What do you do to get what you want? For example, beg, flatter, pressure, and so on.)

CHARACTER TRAITS: (What are you like as a person?)

RELATIONSHIP: (What are your relationships to the other characters?)

OBSTACLES: (What or who stands in the way of your objective?)

EXPLORATION GAMES

Draw a picture of your character(s).

Improvise a scene before the play begins or after it ends.

Dress as your character(s) to see how it changes your behavior.

Make the scene or play into a musical or an opera.

Listen closely to everyone around you during a scene.

Try to make your acting partners respond to your behavior.

Lead with a different body part: in other words, change which part of your body enters the room first and pulls you forward when you walk. Leading with your nose can make you seem pompous, leading with the top of your head can make you seem insecure, etc.

Change the speed/rhythm at which you speak or move.

Decide who you like and who you don't like in the scene; don't be afraid to show it.

Change your volume (whisper or speak out loudly).

Make your voice higher or lower in pitch.

Notice who's taller and who's shorter than you in the scene; let this affect you.

Change your accent.

Sit down with another actor to make up your characters' past lives together.

Do an activity you think your character might do.

Do a chore around the house the way your character might do it.

Write a diary entry, a letter of complaint, or a personal ad as your character.

Come up with a gesture that your character does habitually.

THE AUTHOR

Kristen Dabrowski is an actress, writer, acting teacher, and director. She received her MFA from The Oxford School of Drama in Oxford, England. The actor's life has taken her all over the United States and England. Her other books, published by Smith and Kraus, include *111 Monologues for Middle School Actors Volume 1*, *The Ultimate Audition Book for Teens 3*, *20 Ten-Minute Plays for Teens,* and the *Teens Speak* series. Currently, she lives in the world's smallest apartment in New York City. You can contact the author at monologue madness@yahoo.com.